Joys, Sorrows, and Hopes

Joys, Sorrows, and Hopes

The Life of an African American Family in the Depression-Era South

Grace Marable

iUniverse, Inc.
Bloomington

Joys, Sorrows, and Hopes
The Life of an African American Family in the Depression-Era South

iUniverse books may be ordered through booksellers or by contacting:

iUniverse
1663 Liberty Drive
Bloomington, IN 47403
www.iuniverse.com
1-800-Authors (1-800-288-4677)

ISBN: 978-1-4620-2314-1(pbk)
ISBN: 978-1-4620-2315-8(ebk)

Printed in the United States of America

iUniverse rev. date: 05/25/2011

Table of Contents

Dedication

To the memory of my parents and husband:

Lessie Smedley 1885—1974

Mollie Todd-Smedley 1888—1950

Guy Marable 1925—1989

Acknowledgements

This book—Joys, Sorrows and Hopes—is based on my memories only, not on the memories of others. My sister, Lillie, supplied some names of our father's siblings that I had forgotten. My brother, Oliver, told me in detail how our father stored sweet potatoes away for the winter. This story is as true as I could make it. I used the true names of my parents, grandparents, siblings, nieces and nephews after obtaining their permission.

The process of recalling memories from my childhood to the present, and committing them to paper has been an educational experience for me. At this time, it is for me a form of therapy. The process has allowed me at times to put out of my mind some of the unpleasantness of the present.

After I began writing my life story, my niece Kaye Smedley Wright encouraged me to complete it. I am very appreciative for the encouragement and help she provided. She helped me in the very early stages by bringing her own computer and printer to my home and taught me the basics of using a computer and printer in just one day. She also left instructions for me to study as well as providing instructions over the telephone.

Some months later, my daughter, Gina, gave me a newer computer and printer which were of great benefit to me. Gina helped with much of the typing by taking some of the manuscripts home with her to type which provided me further encouragement. She mailed the manuscript back to me and included a letter that read:

As I was working on the chapters, I laughed and cried. This is such a touching story. It stirred my emotions in so many ways. I understand why you named it Joys, Sorrows and Hopes. Whereas, the general public may find your story interesting, I see your story mainly being of true and lasting value to Stacy, his children, and myself. Especially today, Black children do not have the closeness of the extended family and they therefore have no history on which to reflect. Your story will certainly be of special value to Stacy's children because it will be the only way that they will know of their Smedley roots. Although you may one day sell your autobiography, the true value of your memories cannot be measured. They are worth so much more than mere dollars.

Soon after beginning to write, the public library here in my hometown of Roanoke, Alabama, offered anyone that had interest in writing a life story or autobiography the opportunity to attend an eleven week course entitled—*Reading Our Lives*: A Southern Autobiography Series. I attended each of the classes and found them to be of great benefit.

More encouragement came from a publisher that read a portion of my manuscript. Statements were made that lead me to continue working on my autobiography. Statements such as "I believe you have a wealth of material for a book". Another stated "You are an eloquent witness to an aspect of Alabama history and culture that is not well documented and has not been well understood. I feel that your manuscript is not ready for publication. You write very well and your life story is deserving of a large audience, but successful memories need a narrative structure and descriptive voice that go beyond what you have done so far. Personally, I feel from reading what you have submitted to me that you are quite capable of revising your manuscript to make it more appealing to a general audience. By that, I mean enriching the description, organizing the material better and coming up with a narrative thread that pulls the reader through the material. If you do revise your manuscript, I would be very interested in seeing it again."

An additional source of encouragement came in the form of a letter and a meeting. The letter explained the need to organize the material better so the presentation of it will be effective by including a thematic and chronological combination that would provide coherence. I was encouraged to devote a part of the story to my ancestors including who they were, where they came from and what I knew about their past and their youth. Sharing their background will provide definition and depth into my life story. Lastly, I was encouraged to use my natural storytelling voice.

Childhood and Youth

My name is Grace Smedley Marable. I was born April 5, 1929 in Five Points Alabama to Lessie and Molly Smedley whose only occupation was farming. Five Points Alabama is in Chambers County, and is named for the five roads that meet there. During the nearly eight decades of my life, I have experienced many Joys, Sorrows and Hopes.

I am the youngest of fourteen children born to Lessie and Mollie Smedley, Growing up in a family that size brought some unforgettable experiences. There were sad, happy, fun, dangerous, and exciting times.

Of the fourteen children, there were eleven sons and three daughters. Five of the sons were born first. Theodore was the oldest, followed by Arthur, Taft, Guy and Booker. Then the first daughter was Lillie was born. Then after Lillie, six more sons were born: Barney, Howard, Melvin, Lepolion, Oliver and Donnie. The last two children were girls: Gertrude and myself.

The Lessie & Mollie Todd Smecley Family

Missing Photos: Guv. Howard & Donnie

My parents and eleven of their fourteen children

My earliest memories are of working in the fields even before I began attending school. These memories will cover some of my childhood years, then years as a teenager, young adult, a newlywed, a parent, years as a widow but not necessarily in that order.

We all worked together some of the times, but at other times, maybe two of my brothers worked with the mules in another field while others cut down bushes in another field. Sometimes one or two of my brothers would help Papa cut down the oats and tie them in bundles. After they dried, they were loaded onto the wagon, carried to our barn and stored away to be kept dry. If they ever got wet, they would spoil and the cows and mules could not eat them.

Lessie Smedley or Papa, as we all called our father, was the oldest of seven children, born to Oliver and Fannie Boyd Smedley. They lived in Chambers County, Alabama. In 1898 when Papa had reached thirteen years of age, he and his siblings became orphans after both of his parents had died only two years apart. Grandfather Smedley was a very handsome man who died of an unknown cause, although it is believed that he was murdered by Klansmen.

Grandfather Smedley ca. 1880

In the earlier years of my memories, Papa owned his mules but not the land or the house that we lived in. Papa rented them from a man named Mr. Wheeler. The house we lived in was not a big one; it only had four rooms and a long hallway that separated the rooms. When entering the house from either the front or back porch, you would enter into the hallway. The porch reached all the way across the front of our house. Papa built a swing and a long bench for the front porch and every night in the summer months, after finishing our work we would all sit on the porch before going to bed. It was our place to go and cool off and to get a little rest.

Papa had no picture of Grandmother Smedley. He described her to be a short, brown skinned woman. Papa and his siblings knew very well the reason for their mother's death – she contracted tuberculosis. Papa said that no one they knew ever survived this disease in those days. Grandmother Smedley died in 1898, leaving the seven children orphans.

At the age of thirteen, my father, Lessie Smedley was left with six younger siblings for which to provide – five sisters and one brother. Their names were Ollie, Ina, Eula, Willie, Clara and Ora.

Even before his father died, Papa learned many of the requirements for planting a crop, planting a vegetable garden and planting feed for animals. In those days most children began working in the fields as early as six years old. His mother lived only two years after his father died, so the things that he learned from his father had to be put into practice. Papa and his sisters that were old enough had to do most of the work even before their mother died, since her sickness did not allow her to do much work in the field.

Papa's opportunity to go to school was almost non-existent. He only attended school when it rained, preventing him from working in the field, when it was too cold to cut wood for the fire to warm their house or use in the wood burning stove. Therefore, he only completed the third grade.

After Papa's parents died, he and his siblings lived alone. There was a grandmother who lived nearby. Papa never mentioned whether this was the Smedley or the Boyd grandmother. She was apparently alone because Papa never mentioned a grandfather either. She was unable to care for her grandchildren; it was no doubt all she could do was to care for herself.

Papa provided for himself and siblings by farming someone else's land since his parents had not owned their own farm. He raised cotton to sell, corn and vegetables to eat, and grain for the animals. In addition to the hardships Papa faced as a teenager responsible for six siblings, there was an uncle living with the grandmother who made Papa's life even more difficult. Once when the children had picked the cotton, the uncle took it away. Since Papa was so young, he did not know how to report the theft and could not get it back. However, he continued to work because his sisters and brother depended on the provision from his efforts. Through trial and error, Papa learned how to be an excellent farmer, a practice he continued as he became an old man.

In my mind, I do not picture Papa as being big, because even as an adult he was only five feet, five inches tall and weighed about one hundred and fifty pounds. Despite his small stature, no other man that I knew worked harder than Papa. As far back as I can remember Papa always got up before daybreak whether it was spring, summer, fall or winter. Our house was small – three rooms and a kitchen. My sister Gertrude and I slept in the same room with our parents.

Papa provided for his family by farming, he farmed until he was eighty years old, he never had any type of machinery to help do his farming and he had only tools and instruments that he made. Papa had spent his whole life doing hard manual labor. By the time he reached seventy years of age, he had contracted arthritis in his legs, back, shoulder, arms and hands that caused him excruciating pain.

Both of our parents told us the few things their parents remembered about being freed from slavery. Mama's father, Grandfather Todd, was only nine years old when the slaves were freed and Grandfather Smedley was even younger at that time. They mainly remembered continuing to work in the fields.

Papa and Mama married in 1905 when he was twenty and she was sixteen. Mama's mother died when she was only three and her father, Wash Todd had eighteen children from three different wives. Mama's mother was the first wife and she bore to him six children, five girls and one boy. Mama had one sister younger than herself named Dora. Her older siblings were named Lillie, Carrie, Pearl and their brother was Peter.

After the death of his first wife, Grandfather Todd married again soon afterward to a woman that was very abusive to Mama. With this wife, Grandfather Todd had five sons and one daughter. Of this set of Mama's siblings, I got to know one sister well, dear Aunt Hattie. She was much like another mother to us.

Many times I heard Mama say, "When a man's wife dies, his love for his children dies with her". I worried and was afraid about this when Mama would get sick. I did not understand at the time that she was only referring to some men. I knew that Papa loved me and all of the rest of his children. He protected me from so many things that I was afraid of when I was a child. When Mama's stepmother was mean to her she would go outside into the yard and look up into the sky and ask God to send her mother back to get her. Mama had been told that her mother was in heaven with God and she did not remember her mother very well but did not think her real mother would be mean to her. She said it was years later that she learned from studying the bible that her mother was not in heaven with God and was still in her grave waiting for God's time to resurrect the dead.

Grandfather Todd ca. 1870

Grandfather Todd's second wife died sometime later, and then he married a third wife. Six children were born to that union, four sons and two daughters. The daughters were named Anna Laura and Emily; the sons were Hutchinson, Julius, Woodrow, and Boolum.

My father was a brown skinned man and I inherited my color from him, but not his hair texture. His hair did not curl up as mine does; with most of my ancestry being black, it's not surprising that my hair and color are different from my parents. I have my mom's exact body build, but grew to be a few inches taller than she was. Mama sometimes said to me, "Grace, I believe you are going to be six feet tall". Mama had sisters that were almost six feet and I grew to be only five feet and six inches tall.

Mama spent many hours sewing for different white ladies. When the ladies came to our house to pick up whatever Mama had made for them, many times they asked, "Mollie, how do you keep this house so clean with all the children you have?" Mama's reply was, "Everyone, little or big works to help me". Mama worked equally as hard as Papa did. She worked along in the fields with us and she sewed most of our clothes and mended them when needed.

The way we cleaned our house was very different from the way they clean houses today. None of our walls were painted and no rugs were used on the floors except the area rugs that Mama made. To make the rugs, long strips of material were cut from old no longer wearable garments and strips that were left from new garments. Mama then braided these long strips together and would ask me or one of the other children to hold the end of the strips while she braided. It took many hours to make enough braids for a rug. Mama then sewed the braids in a circle by hand. Sometimes she formed the rugs in a circle, other times she made the rugs oblong. She made them to lie beside our beds so that when we got up in the morning our feet would be warm.

When it was time to clean the walls and ceiling, we would take everything in a room outside except for the bed frame them we would wash everything down with boiling hot water and home made lye soap. Mama would throw water against the walls and ceiling to clean them. Mama would always throw the water because she said that if she let one of us children do it, we might burn ourselves. My brother brought the tubs of water in the house for Mama to use. When every room was finished and dried, the furniture was brought back into the house. The rooms was so pleasant to smell, the washing of the rooms were done once a year. To clean the floors, Papa made a mop out of corn shucks. We used white sand and water to scrub the floors, because Mama said soap on the floors will turn the floors dark and using sand kept them almost white.

Today, I watch home shows on the television to get new ideas for decorating or redecorating my home. Mama's work methods for decorating the house were original; I learn creative ways of cleaning the house by watching television. Mama got some of her ideas from the *Sears and Roebuck* catalog, but she had no instructions to follow. It was a matter of looking at pictures and guessing as to how it was done. Mama got some recipes out of magazines and papers that came in the mail. She would prepare some new dishes from them but most of the food she prepared she used her own recipe. She would often make delicious peach, apple or black berry cobbler that almost made it possible for us to forget what our day had been like.

Mama loved flowers and enjoyed working with them in the garden, watching them grow and seeing the pretty blooms they produced. Papa built Mama a flower box across one end of the porch. Mama planted only one kind of flowers in it, different colors of petunias. They grew and bloomed so pretty for many months until the frost came. Those petunias trailed down the sides of the box until the box could no longer be seen from the front or the back. It looked like a large bed of flowers. Dozens of butterflies of all colors and sizes flew all over the blooms. Our neighbors always admired those flowers.

In our front yard Papa always plowed up a big flower bed for Mama, Gertrude and I to plant our flower seeds that we had saved from the year before. They grew and had beautiful blooms on them. Mama cut some of the blooms and made arrangements from them for the inside of our house. In the summertime our windows were always open so that fresh air and the fragrance from the flowers made our house smell nice.

Every afternoon Mama would remind one of my brothers to draw some water from the well to water the petunias. The box was partly under the roof and could not always get watered from the rain.

Gertrude and I had lots of fun playing with our brothers. Since we were the youngest girls, they were always told not to hurt us. They never did hurt us really bad. Melvin was not having fun unless he was hurting someone just a little bit. He made for himself these funny looking wagons to play with and just begged Gertrude and me to let him carry us for a ride in it. He always promised not to let it turn over. We got in the wagon for a few minutes and everything was fine but when he got close to a ditch it always turned over and he always found it to be so funny but did not know how that happened. It never hurt us, only scared us we always ran home and would tell Mama what Melvin had done. She reminded us that we knew that he would do that just why do you always believe him, we would say "Mama, but he promised not to do it again".

Melvin not only had fun treating us that way, he found ways to get our other brothers in trouble or hurt them some way. I cannot even remember Melvin getting punished for his ways. I suppose our parents thought that one day we would learn not to play with him. I don't think any of us ever did learn.

I don't have many memories of my brother Guy. Guy and his wife Irene moved into a house that was about five miles from ours. Once when Gertrude was only five years old, she stayed overnight with them but the next morning when she asked them to take her home they couldn't do it right away so she left without telling anyone. When she got home, Papa and Mama got so upset with Guy and Irene for letting her walk home alone. Mama said over and over to her "You are only five years old and you should not have come that long way alone. Some bad man could have hurt you". Gertrude told Mama "I asked God to take care of me until I got to you and he did".

My next earliest memories are of Guy's wife having their second son. Mama took me with her one day to help Irene with her baby and while we were there Guy came home from work. I asked him where that baby came from and he told me that he got it out of a tree stump in the woods. I was only five years old but I knew that he was fooling me but I never asked him anything else about it. After Guy and his family later moved to West Virginia to get a job I don't remember seeing him again until many years later although Mama and Papa went to West Virginia occasionally to visit my siblings who lived there.

When I was very young, Gertrude and I would have to stay home from school in the springtime when Papa was starting the crop for that year. When the time came for Papa to get the field ready for planting cotton, the dead cotton stalks from the year before were still standing in the field. We stayed home from school to cut those stalks down with a hoe. We would then pick up the stalks and put them in piles that Papa would burn. That would take us about two weeks to complete and then we would start attending school again.

If Papa was not in the field with us, he would be working in the garden getting all of the vegetables that we needed planted. He kept all of the weeds and grass round the fruit trees cut down and pruned them properly at the right time of year. Some of the vegetables seeds Papa bought from the peddler and some he saved from the garden the year before. We always had a big pretty vegetable garden. I think that every vegetable Papa had knowledge of that grew in the south he planted. Our garden was always close to the house and it was fenced in so that rabbits, squirrels, chickens or dogs couldn't get into it. Down in the field a short distance from the garden is where most of the fruit trees grew, except one big pear tree and one pomegranate tree that was close to the house. A persimmon tree grew in the cow pasture and we had a grapevine in our yard as well. He also repaired the pasture fences when they need it.

Papa did not put commercial fertilizers in the garden. He used manure from the chicken house and the cow's pen. He told us that fertilizers were good to make corn and cotton grow but made the vegetables unhealthy for us.

11

In the winter months our parents were just as busy as they were in the spring. We used fireplaces that burned wood and a wood heater to heat our house. Papa would go into the woods in the pasture and cut down trees and unload them at the edge of the yard. That made it possible for us to always have wood to burn when the weather was cold.

In the morning when it was cold weather, Papa would first start a fire in all the bedroom fireplaces except for the boy's room, Papa would then start a fire in the kitchen stove to make coffee for breakfast. Mama would rise soon after Papa and join him in the kitchen. She would start mixing together flour, milk, soda, baking powder, salt and shortening to make biscuits from scratch everyday.

While it was still dark outside, Papa would draw water from the will to use in the kitchen and water so we could bathe and get ready for school. By that time, my brothers were out of bed and busy making a fire in their room. They would then join Papa outside to help him feed the cows, mules, hogs and chickens. By the time all of that was done, breakfast would be ready. We always ate breakfast together. After breakfast, Mama and I would go to the barn and milk the cows. Gertrude stayed inside and cleaned the kitchen. We then got dressed and went to school. These early morning activities by no means ended Papa's working day.

Many times my hands and feet would be so cold when I got home. Mama was always ready and waiting to warm them with a pan of warm water for me to hold my hands in for a few minutes. I remember the water feeling so good. My feet would be warmed by putting the pan on the floor for me to put my feet in.

Girls did not wear pants or jeans to school in the nineteen thirties and forties, at least not the school that we attended. We walked about four miles to school and Mama believed that if our legs were not covered during that long walk in the cold weather, we would have rheumatism in our joints when we got older. So in October, she would order thick ribbed cotton stockings for Gertrude and me. She also ordered cotton knit underwear that buttoned down the front and reached our knees. I did not mind wearing the underwear but I wanted to wear socks as some of the other little girls did. I begged Mama at times to let me wear socks. Mama would then ask me "Do you want to be crippled when you get old and have to walk with a stick?" That would always end my begging. Time has obviously proven Mama to be correct. Today, I am nearly seventy years old and have no problems with my joints.

When I began attending school, I was already seven years old. I never asked why I was not sent to school at six. The first school that I attended started children off in a grade called the primer instead of first grade. I don't remember disliking school. I must have been shy at the start of school because I didn't talk to my teacher if I could avoid it. That shyness did not last very long. While still in elementary school, I started to like the little boys and enjoyed playing with them more than the little girls at playtime at school. One little boy was special to me. I would write him a letter everyday. Whenever I had to miss school for any reason, it made me very unhappy.

School buses were not provided for black children in Alabama at that time so we walked to and from school. I wondered why the white children had buses to ride in and we did not. Crossing the cow pasture, making our way through the woods and getting across the creek did not end our problems. We walked on a dirt road after leaving school for about one half of a mile then we left the road and took a path through a cow pasture. At times, a bull inside the pasture did not want us there. The older children walking along with us collected rocks and sticks to fight him away from us. Once we got through the pasture and away from the cows by crawling on the ground to get under the wire fence that was around the pasture. A creek ran through the woods where the water rushed though as if it was in a great hurry to get to its destination. We had to cross over that creek on a huge log that provided the only means to cross. Other children, like me, who were in our first years of school, were

13

terrified at the thought of having to walk on the log over the water. The water running under the log was hitting against the rocks sounded angry to me. To make it bearable to cross, Papa nailed planks to the log and tired wire to the planks creating something to hold onto while walking across the log. With the wire to hold onto and my brother holding my hand I was safe.

When we got back to the road, as we continued on our way home, the bus carrying the white children would come by. We would leave the road and run into the fields to get away from the children hanging out of the windows and throwing rocks at us. When we walked home, even the sound of a truck would frighten us. We thought that maybe it was the bus carrying the white children home and we may need to run into the field. I was always afraid of how much it would hurt if I were hit by a rock. When we told Mama and Papa what happened, their advice was to watch out for the bus and get out of their reach but there was no explanation of why they did that.

My parents did not go into any details about the horrible way black people were treated in those days. They did not want us treated that way because they knew that it wasn't right. The fact that my parents were born in the south, in the eighteen hundreds probably meant that they had similar or even worse experiences that they did not talk about with their children.

Walking to school every day caused our shoes to soon wear out and needed to be repaired. Papa repaired our shoes with leather that he saved from the cows hides when he killed a cow for us to eat. He would hang the hides in the barn to dry out. When the hide was dry enough to work with, he cut it into pieces and repaired our shoes and made it possible for us to continue to walk to school.

Since it was so many of us to buy shoes for, they could only buy us one pair of shoes each for the school year. When it was no longer possible to repair my shoes, Mama would give me her shoes to wear so I could continue to attend school. I cannot remember what Mama would wear after she gave me her shoes. I do remember that our Aunt Hattie sent us a box every year during the winter months. We were always happy to receive the big box with clothes, shoes and other things in it. We could hardly wait to open that box when it arrived from Aunt Hattie. She worked for some rich white people in Indianapolis, Indiana. They always let her send us the clothes that they were not going to wear any longer.

I get sad remembering that Mama had to go outside in the winter to wash our clothes, to get water from the well to use inside for cooking, bathing, drinking and scrubbing floors. If Papa were home, he would get the water for her but many times he had work to do away from home.

Mama was the prettiest and busiest woman in the world to me. When she was not working in the field with us, she would be home cooking, cleaning, washing, ironing, sewing or doctoring on someone's hurt toe, foot, leg arm or maybe even someone's hurt feelings. Her sewing including making area rugs for the floors, bed covers, curtains, wash clothes and towels. When Papa bought fertilizer for the crops in sacks, she reused the sacks to sew things for our house. She would wash the sacks in boiling water in an iron wash pot and then hang them on the clothes line for days. The sun helped to whiten them, then Mama would unravel the strings from the sacks and each sack equaled to a little over one yard of material.

Papa and Mama had very little formal schooling. Mama completed the fourth grade and inherited her light skin color and soft curly hair from her mulatto parents who were children of their slave masters. Two different white men owned her parents.

Mama read every book that she could get her hands on. Many times after reading a book or magazine, she told us what she had read about. (Some of the books that she read came from the white family named Prather that lived near us.) The titles of other books include: "The truth shall make you free", published in 1943, "Government", published in 1928, "Life" published in 1929 and "Let God be true", published in 1946. She read the Bible and the Bible study aids named above also. She regularly read copies of the Watchtower and Awake magazines, which I continue to read to this day.

We were poor, like most black people in those days. But we had the necessary food, clothing and shelter. Regarding 'Love and Togetherness', I realize that we had much more at that time, than most people have today. I cannot remember a time coming home from school when Mama wasn't there. She was always there with our food ready and waiting for us.

The food that Mama prepared for us always smelled so good. We appreciated the sweet potatoes, turnips, peas, beans or whatever she had prepared. Many times when it was really cold, Mama prepared a big pot of stew of some kind and a delicious peach, apple or black berry cobbler that almost made it possible for us to forget what our day had been like.

I don't only have sad memories of my childhood; there are many more happy ones. When we were children we made most of our toys. That was fun because Mama and Papa helped us or showed us how to make toys. Things like wagons, cars, dolls and doll clothes. We tried to make most of the toys we saw in the Sears & Roebuck catalog because we didn't have enough money to buy any of them.

Some of the games that we played in the winter months at home were so different from games that children play today. Mama made what she called fire balls for us. She took old clothes that had worn out and rolled it up into a ball, tied it with strings and soaked it with the kerosene that we used in our lamps for light at night. The ball soaked with kerosene was put near a fire to light it. We threw it to each other as we stood in a circle and no one ever got burned. The fire ball looked so pretty flying in the dark.

Other times, our neighbors joined us and took pieces of wood and broken off tree limbs into an open field. At night, the men piled all the wood and tree limbs up as high as they could reach and then set fire to it. We were not allowed to go near it, but we ran around the barn fire playing ring games which were so much fun. If those games were played today, someone would surely get burned or hurt somehow. Our parents always stayed right there with us. I suppose that is why none of us ever got hurt.

One of the stories that we talked about for years in our family was about Gertrude going home with Aunt Dora who was one of Mama's sisters who lived in Birmingham Alabama. She was given a pair of skates while she was there and she brought them home with her. Every summer my brothers tried to make themselves skates to play with. They searched and found some old wheels and pieces of boards, they nailed that together to make what they called skates. We had lot of fun just trying to ride what they had made.

Once Gertrude and I left the field to go and pick some berries to eat. To get to the berry vines we had to cross a ditch which was not very wide but it was deep, and we both knew it. I was never as brave as Gertrude, so I told her I would go further down the field to where the ditch was not as deep and cross there. She told me, "Grace, wait and let me show you how easy it is to cross this ditch right here". She walked back a few feet from the ditch to get a running start to jump over the ditch. When she tried to jump, part of the bank caved in; and down into the ditch she went, completely out of sight. I just knew she was dead and I didn't even look down to see her. I ran to Papa as fast as I could, crying all of the way. When I reached him, I told him what had happened. He ran back to the ditch with me and when we got there Gertrude was just getting out of the ditch. She told us that she climbed out by the vines in the ditch. I was still so upset; Papa was trying to comfort me even after I could see she was alright.

Our swimming pool was a creek that ran through the pasture. All of my brothers could swim but I could not. It was lots of fun just playing in the water. The water was always running as if it were coming off of a hill. Papa told us children to always play in the running water because it was cleaner than the standing water. Occasionally, there would be a snake swimming down the creek. When we would see it, we just stepped to the side and let it keep going on its way.

I don't ever remember going in the cow pasture without seeing some type of snake. If the sakes were not in the water and my brothers were around, they didn't stand a chance of surviving. My older brothers treated snakes really bad. If they saw one that was not poisonous, they caught it, held it down on the ground, then pinned its mouth shut with a safety pin, then they would let it go. I didn't personally see my older brothers do this, my parents told me about it later.

Papa and my brothers would use old car and truck tires to make swings for us to play on. A rope would run through the tire and then be tied to a tree limb. The tire was then hanging from the tree that was now a swing for us. We had a lot of fun pushing each other on it. Sometimes other children who lived near by would play with us. Being a part of a large family, we always had someone to play with when not working in the field.

I was a bout eight years old when we got a radio. It was powered by a battery, since we did not have electricity in our house. It was a big radio that was ordered from Sears and Roebuck for $39.99, which was a lot of money for us. My siblings that worked away from home put their money together and sent most of the money that was used to buy it. The batteries lasted only so many hours so when we children were home during the day, we rarely turned the radio on to make the batteries last longer.

We enjoyed listening to country music at night. Mama liked to listen to the soaps during the day, especially Stella Dallas. Stella Dallas was a 15 minute soap opera that ran from 1937 to 1955 and was the story of a poor farmhand who married a rich man named Stephen Dallas; her strong love for her daughter Laurel was the primary theme of the series.

One summer, something happened that frightened me so much that I will never forget it. I was carrying water to Papa and Barney to drink in the field where they were working. I heard this strange noise that was caused by a zeppelin flying in the sky.

I had seen an airplane, maybe once or twice, but had never seen a zeppelin. Seeing it and hearing the noise frightened me so that I started screaming and couldn't even move. Papa had to run across the field to pick me up and carry me home.

When we went to church at night we always rode in the wagon pulled by two mules. We walked to church in the daytime. There were two bridges between our house and the church that we had to cross. The bridges were built of wooden planks spaced so far apart that I could see the water running under it. I thought that I could fall through the cracks, so Papa always had to pick me up and carry me across.

I know that I was at times a burdensome child to my parents. In my mind, I see this little girl who was not the least bit pretty, big for my age and whose hair was never pretty to me because it did not look like my mom's. Once, Mama was combing my hair and I told her that she was hurting me. Mama said "I'm sorry, I don't mean to hurt you. I'm just trying to make your hair look nice". I told her "You do mean to hurt me, because you do not like me because I have nappy hair". Mama didn't say another word to me. When I looked in her face, she was crying with tears running down her face. My words were so mean that to this day, I wish I would have apologized and told Mama that I was sorry and that I did not mean it.

Dogs

Living on a farm, we always had animals around. There were work animals as well as the ones kept to slaughter for food. And of course there were the pets. For us kids, our dogs were most important. One very smart dog named Ned was particularly important to us and we still speak of him today.

Late in the afternoons we always milked our cows. After putting the food out for them, one of us kids had to go a short distance down the road to open the pasture fence gate so the cows could come out of the pasture. Once they came out, most of the time they just walked straight to the barn. Other times they acted stubborn. All we had to do was say, "Ned, get the cows". He rounded them up and straight to the gate they came running and didn't stop running until they got inside of the barnyard.

If one of us kids were due for a punishment from either of our parents, neither one could whip us outside because Ned would not allow it. Our parent's way of punishing us was whoever was in trouble would have to go to the peach tree and get a limb that was to be used as a switch. We were told that our legs were about to be stung with the switch. Ned would take the switch away. If either parent was determined to do it, we had to be carried inside away from Ned's view.

We kept Ned for a long time and then one night he disappeared. Papa and my brothers looked for him for days but never found him.

We missed him and continued to hope that one day he would come home but he never did. Mama and Papa assumed that some white people probably stole him because they would constantly offer to buy Ned but they would never sell him. We had another dog at the time but his main concern was only when he would be fed. He was always just lying around the kitchen door.

Around that time is when someone gave my brother Melvin a puppy. We always named our dogs but I cannot remember the name that Melvin gave the dog. I do not even remember if it was a male or female. That puppy was Melvin's companion. After some months this puppy grew up and got sick. We never took our dogs to a doctor and I don't think that during those times no one ever gave their dogs any shots.

Melvin began giving this dog whatever medicine we gave one of the other dogs when they got sick. The dog never got better but began to dislike every one of us. He had contacted rabies. Ou parents assumed that he had infected five of us kids, including myself. From our parents thought Melvin was infected because of the close contact he had with the dog. My sister Lillie was thought to be infected by a scratch on her leg. One day when she was sweeping our back yard, the dog was determined to take the broom away from her but she did not allow him to and got scratched.

One day after the dog began to act strangely, Gertrude was eating a stalk of sugar cane the dog started chasing her for no reason. She fought him off with the stalk of cane until she reached a bale of cotton and climbed on it. He went away since he could not climb that high. She continued to eat that stalk of cane was thought to be infected as well.

That same day I went outside none of us realizing what was wrong he ran to me and fastened his mouth around my leg and tore the flesh about an inch. After he bit me he left home and disappeared. My parents were afraid that he had "gone mad", as we referred to rabies in those days. They talked to the mailman Mr. Smith who advised them to find the dog if at all possible. Mr. Smith would at times talk to Papa for a while before continuing on with his route. If Mama needed to mail a letter and she did not have the money for the postage, she would put one or two eggs in the mailbox with the letters. Mr. Smith would take the eggs and put the stamps on the mail. Mr. Smith was a kind white man that my parents must have trusted to ask for advice regarding the dog that had contracted rabies.

After looking for the dog for some days, they found it not too far from our house. Mr. Smith then advised them to carry the dog to our family doctor who lived about three miles for us. Dr. Piper would know what needed to be done. The first thing was to find out if the dog had rabies. Dr. Piper sent the dogs head to Montgomery, Alabama for an autopsy. The dog did indeed have the rabies germ. Medicine was sent to Dr. Piper with which to treat us. Our treatments were to take twenty shots, each in the stomach, over a period of twenty days.

Those shots killed whatever germ we had contacted from the dog, because none of use got the least bit sick afterward. When our parents were sure we were going to be alright, mama said many nights she had dreamed that all of her children had gone mad just as the dog did. I can only imagine the burden and worry that was on her.

Going to Dr. Piper's house every day was a scary event. Not the trip itself because we traveled our usual way when going away from home. Papa hitched the mules to the wagon and we all climbed aboard. The scary time was the late afternoon appointments that we had everyday with Dr. Piper. Papa drove the wagon into Dr., Piper's yard and fastened the mules to one of the trees in the yard. Once that was done, Papa and Mama escorted one of us at a time from the wagon up to the doctor's porch. His bag was on the porch but he walked down the steps and gave us the shots standing near the porch on the ground. When it was my turn to get the shot, both Mama and Papa had to hold me still. The shots in the stomach were very painful. The doctor told me that he would put me in jail if I kicked him.

That experience didn't affect our love for dogs. I do remember that afterward when and if a dog of ours got sick, Papa fastened it up in a pen and he took care of it. None of us was allowed near it until it was well and out of the confined place.

By the time the ordeal with the rabid dog was over, it had involved about two months of worry, fear and anxiety for our parents. Before this happened and afterward if one of us got sick and needed a doctor, Dr. Piper came to our house to treat us. Papa always rode one of his mules to the doctor's house to explain our symptoms.

My parents knew that when a dog got rabies that this was serous and dangerous and if a person got rabies they would die. They had reminded us kids if you see a strange dog in the road to try not to let the dog get near us. They told us if you cannot get inside of the house, climb up the nearest tree that you can get to or climb to the top of a fence and stay there until the dog goes away. Our parents knew also that the dog would die soon if it had rabies.

Our Move to Mr. Avery's Farm

I was about ten years old and was still sleeping in the same room with our parents. It was necessary since it was about seven of us children still at home. When we moved to our new place we had the same sleeping arrangements. One night before we moved, I was awakening by the sound of Mama and Papa's voices but the tone of their voices were so different. Mama sounded as if she was crying. Papa was trying to comfort her by telling her not to worry herself sick and that he would somehow find us some place to live.

They had been told by Mr. Wheeler, the owner of the place where we were then living to move away from his farm. The reason was we were not making enough cotton, corn or anything else to please him on his land. Mr. Wheeler took everything that we grew on the farm that year, including the mules, cows and hogs. He did allow us to keep one heifer. He did to us what they called "cleaning you up". That heifer that he let us keep was pregnant at the time. I suppose Mr. Wheeler's heart would not let him send us away without anything.

Papa told Mama that he would find us another farm to live on and that farm house belonged to Mr. Avery. When we moved to our new farm it was wintertime. Our moving away from Mr. Wheeler's farm was the second move from him. My parents had rented a farm from him once before, but that was before I was born. Black people did not own land and houses at least not many did. Getting a job some other place was just about out of the questions. If my father had work anyplace, it would have been working for wages on someone else's farm for a few dollars a month.

My brother Barney, worked for wages, as it was called for a while. He earned ten dollars a month. He worked from sun up to sun down, six days a week. He picked cotton, planted cotton, planted and pulled corn, and stored the corn in the owner's barn. He did whatever needed to be done on the man's farm.

When just about everything was taken from us, we did not even have a wagon left, he took that too. To be farmers it is necessary to own a wagon. I said he took everything but that is not exactly true. When you live on a farm the way we did, all of your material needs must come from the farm. When the vegetables in the garden were ready, we gathered bushels of beans, peas, corn, turnips, okra, squash, tomatoes and whatever else we grew, Mama canned the vegetables in glass jars, preserved the fruits, she dried some of the fruit canned some of it also. She did this so that we had food to eat during the winter months when nothing grew. Mr. Wheeler took none of this from us.
All the cows except one heifer was taken away from us, we no longer had milk to drink nor butter to eat anymore. Yes, we had plenty to eat but never in my life before did we not have milk to drink every day for breakfast, dinner and supper. Our parents thought it was absolutely necessary for children to have milk everyday. At an early age is when I began drinking coffee every morning.

After we lived at this place for a while, Mama asked the white lady that lived just up the road a short distance from us if she could come to her house everyday and churn her milk for her, for one gallon of milk a day. The lady agreed for her to do that. We now had milk again to drink.

After Mama cooked our breakfast that always included hot biscuits along with whatever else we were having, she would see to Gertrude and I getting started cleaning the kitchen up. Mama then got a one gallon jug and up the hill she would go to churn for that lady. I do not remember her name, but she had a little girl and boy about my age that Gertrude and I played with sometimes.

When getting to the house Mama always had to enter the house from the back door. The kitchen was on the back. Mama was not there to visit, and in the 1940s, it was the custom for black people to enter through the back door of a white person's home.

Mama's main concern was to obtain a gallon of milk. After she churned the milk and all the butter had come to the top of the milk, she dipped the butter off the milk, and then poured a small amount of water over it to rinse away any milk that was clinging to it. She then added a small amount of salt to the butter, shaped it into a pretty cake like design, with wax paper and put it in the lady's refrigerator; all except that one gallon she gave to Mama. Entering the house from the back did not worry Mama. She would have been willing to churn milk in the back yard if that was what it took to get the milk she needed for her children.

Mama then washed the churn, the dasher and lid and put them away. The milk she had worked for she brought home stopped at the well drew water poured it into a small tub and put the gallon of milk in it. We did not own a refrigerator there was no electricity in our house. So putting the milk in fresh water made it cool and it tasted better that way. Mama used the milk for cooking and before the day was gone that gallon of milk was used up.

By 1940 there were only six of us kids living at home during the week but on the weekends there were eight of us home. Two brothers that worked away from home came home every Saturday and Sunday.

In the summer of 1940 two county agents began visiting the homes of families who farmed. They came to teach us ways to use everything that we grew on the farm to our best benefit. Mama's way of canning fruits and vegetables was a very slow process. The food would be packed in pint, quart and one half gallon size jars, and then put in the wash pot in water. Each jar had been sealed well and boiled in this water for many hours. Those county agents brought to our house big pressure cookers and taught us how to use them. Before canning food our original way the food in the jars sometimes spoiled because as the jars in the iron wash pot bumped against each other causing the seal of the jar tops to break. Air then got inside, causing spoilage to some of the food. Once we began using those pressure cookers no spoilage occurred.

Until those county agents visited us, all the mattresses were used on our beds were made at home and had loose cotton in them. When Papa carried a load of cotton to the cotton gin to be made into bales, the seeds were separated from the cotton which had to be done in order to make it into a bale. Papa was allowed to take out some of the cotton for home use. Those county agents taught us how to make mattress very similar to the way they are made today and we did it all by hand.

First of all, a frame was built large enough to hold a mattress. The tick fabric used to make the mattress was laid flat and straight on the frame. The cotton was laid on the fabric very evenly and piled up to about twelve inches high. The top piece of fabric was laid on top of the piled cotton. We had needles that were twelve to fourteen inches long. We used them to tack the mattresses. The needles were pushed through the fabric and cotton. One of us kids stationed ourselves under the frame so that when the needle came through it was caught pulled completely through the fabric, thread and all. The needle was then moved over about one half inch and pushed back up through the cotton. The person working on the top pulled it through, tied it in a tight knot cut the thread and moved over about four inches from the tacked one and continued until the tacking was completed.

Sleeping on those tacked mattress were much cooler in the summer than the loose cotton soft ones. The original ones were left on our beds and the new tacked ones put on the top of it. Making up the beds every day was Gertrude's and my job. That made getting the beds arranged so much easier for us. Even when we were little girls if we did not work with the loose cotton until it was even and smooth. Mama always said to take the sheets and spread off the bed and work with the cotton again because you did not make it look nice.

All farm owners did not allow cotton to be saved for home use. Some families used corn shucks and some used straw from the fields to make mattress for their beds. Some of my friends from school had that type of bed. When I spent the night with them, I experienced sleeping on them. When I got back home after a night away from home our loose cotton mattress felt really good.

The heifer that we were able to keep gave birth to her calf later that spring. We were happy when she gave birth now we had all the milk we needed and butter as well. Mama always made biscuits for breakfast. We opened them while they were still hot and put a slice of butter inside the hot biscuit with some straw berry preserve that Mama had made plus a glass of milk was so good to me.

Last winter a neighbor gave me two beautiful white Japanese silky chickens, one male and one female. I named them and was looking forward to raising some young ones from them. I had raised chickens before but for some reason those reminded me of some chickens that Mama and Papa had raised. Maybe it was because they were white and I had to keep them fastened up in a wire cage. If I let them out, my chow dog would chase them in the back yard.

My parents once raised white chickens and they kept them fastened up. Part of the housing for them was a wire cage that was built up about twelve inches from the ground. They kept those chicks until they weighed only two pounds, then they were sold to a chicken market.

Someone came to our house and picked them up, paid my parents for them and took them away. Before leaving our house they left more baby chick to be raised, usually no more than fifty chick each time. They were kept in a two compartment chicken cage. That cage accommodated only fifty chicks at a time.

The instruction for building the housing for the chicks was given to my father by a county agent. The two compartments were connected together, one was for the chick to roost in at night. It was built about twelve inches up from the ground. The sides and top was made out of wood but the floor was built out of galvanized tin. Two 100 watt light bulbs were kept burning at night to keep the chicks warm. It also allowed them to continue eating at night. My parent's purpose was for those baby chickens to weigh two pounds within six weeks if possible. The sooner they got them to the proper weight, the more per pound they were paid for them. The other part of the chicken pen was called a sun porch. The sides, bottom and top was built of wire only the frame was built out of wood.

Playing in our yard with my sister Gertrude in the playhouse that Papa built for us, we had many happy times. The house was just large enough for the two of us to get in and we loved that house. Papa built us a little stove out of some tin that was lying around. The stove was used for cooking for our dolls. He built a little table for our dolls also. Gertrude and I made beds for our baby dolls in the playhouse. The food we prepared for our dolls were mud pies made in large jar lids and grass placed in old cans for their vegetables. We spent hours playing in the house.

It seems like only a short time ago that I would hear Mama call either Melvin, Oliver, Lepolion, Donnie or Barney to draw her some water from the well and fill the tubs and the wash pots so that she could wash our clothes. There was always so much to wash since we got really dirty working in the fields. Papa and Mama both were very clean people and would not allow us to wear dirty clothes if we were not working in the field.

Other black families who lived on Mr. Avery's farm warned us that he would come to the field when we were at work and just stand there and watch us work. My parents said if he does that to us we will just leave the field and go home until he left. Then we would go back to work, he never came to our field to watch us, not one time.

Papa rented this farm with the desire in mind to work hard and keep the field clean from any weeds growing that might have hindered the cotton, corn and other crop from growing the way it needed to. The crops needed also to be dug and plowed around that kept the soil from packing down and to prevent growth.

The days were long and the weather hot. By the middle of the afternoon, we were all so hot and tired but we continued to work until almost sundown. We were then dirty and wet from sweating from our head to our toes. Our clothes were just sticking to our bodies. We left the field near sundown, though our working was not finished for the day. The cows had to be fed and milked. The chickens and hogs had to be fed, the eggs to be gathered and the mules fed.

Before we went back to the field everyday after our dinner, we filled the wash tubs with water from the well, set them out in the sun, so when we finished working the water in the tubs would be warmed by the sun so we could take a bath after eating our supper. Because of being so tired we all went to bed and to me the next day always came quickly.

If we were working in the field, either chopping cotton, picking cotton and Papa was working with us and a bad cloud came up and it was about to rain, we all wanted to leave the field to go home. So we wouldn't get wet once the rain started. Papa did not let us leave until the rain started. The reason he gave was that the rain might not come or the clouds might rain out before getting to us. If we go home now we will just be wasting time. We couldn't even leave if there was thundering and lightning. I was afraid of the noise the thunder made and thought the lightning might strike me that way it struck a tree in our cow pasture.

Sometimes Mama called to us saying, "come home please, before it starts to rain. If you get wet, I will have all those clothes to wash again". That was a time Papa allowed us to leave before the rain came. I thought Papa was just being mean to us, but as I grew older I realized he was not, but instead, he was trying to make the good crop that we so desperately needed. However, it did not always turn out to be so.

Sometimes I wanted to play in the sand making sand piles and sand tunnels. I so wanted to sit on the ground. Mama let us play in the sand but we could not sit on the ground. She said our clothes would get dirty. She said, "Grace, the white people say colored people are always dirty, but we are clean colored people".

There were times during watermelon season that one of us would have to go to the peach trees and get a limb from it, because one of us had gotten watermelon juice on our clothes. We were told to eat our melons with a spoon or a fork so the juice would not drip down on our clothes. If you put a piece of watermelon up to your moth holding with two hands, the juice dripped down your arm and onto our clothes and for that we got a whipping with peach tree limb. I never went to Mama if I was the one due for the punishment. I would run away and hid from her. She sent my brothers to find me. They carried me back to her kicking and screaming. I don't remember getting many whippings when I was a little girl. Sometimes Mama said "Grace, if I was not so tired I would whip you for that". I was happy that she was too tired.

Watching Papa eat his food when I was a little girl amazed me and was very interesting to me. He ate different from the rest of us. We were taught when we were children to eat our food with either a fork or spoon. Papa used his knife, fork and spoon and never touched any of his food with his hands. One example is if it was breakfast time and we were having biscuits, some kind of meat and scrambled eggs. Papa always first thanked God for our food before we started eating. When he began to eat, he picked up his knife and fork. He used the knife to cut a piece of the bread, then picked-up that piece with his fork and put it in his mouth. He then cut a piece of meat in the same way picking it up with his fork as he did the bread. Watching him, I sometimes said to myself, 'Papa will not use a knife to cut that scrambled egg', but he did and carefully picked it up with the fork. When he finished eating his plate was almost clean. Some of the grandchildren watched him as he ate, but no one ever said one word to him about his method of eating.

The Dinner Bell – and a Tragedy

I remember a sound from so long ago that was so pleasing to my ears. The sound was from our dinner bell. At 11:30a.m., everyday that we worked in the fields, Mama would ring it. That was to let us know that dinner was ready and we should come home. That bell was an essential part of our routine of life on the farm. I do not remember a time when it was not in our yard. It was always there and used. When the bell was put in our yard, Papa nailed it to a tall post with a rope tied to the top of the bell. The rope was long enough to be reached from the ground by Mama. When she pulled on it, it caused the bell to swing from one side to the other. The bell was made of iron and was at least two feet high and very heavy. A round iron ball hung down inside of it. As the rope was pulled, the ball hit one side of the bell and then the other. The ranging of the bell could be heard for many miles away. When we moved from one place to another, Papa took the bell and the post down and they moved along with us. When Papa stopped farming he let the bell continue to hang on the tall post in the back yard.

More than twenty hears ago, my sister took our dinner bell home with her to Columbus, Ohio. It was at the time still hanging on a post in Papa's back yard. She asked Papa for it and he gave it to her. Lillie's husband installed it on a post for her in the back yard. A few months ago Oliver took it down for her because she and her husband were selling their home to move into a senior citizens apartment for health reasons.

Oliver lives in Ohio, so when he came to my home to visit, I asked him to bring the bell to me if he did not want it in his yard. He brought it to me. I had planned to have it put up in my yard. Finally I did have the bell put up in my back yard.

When Oliver brought the bell to me, so many memories came with it. Many happy ones because every day it was a reminder that we could stop working in the fields for a while and that now we were about to have some of Mama's good cooking. Other memories surfaced that were different.

One day in 1940 Papa sent Lepolion and Donnie to a field for a long distance from our house to do some plowing with two of the mules. By this time we were living on Mr. Avery's farm and the mules belonged to him. At eleven thirty, Mama rang the bell for all of us to come to dinner. Some of us were chopping cotton in another field, Papa and some of my other brothers were working some other place. We all went home to eat dinner except for Lepolion and Donnie. They had to carry the mules to Mr. Avery's barn to feed and water them before coming home.

As they had done before, Lepolion climbed upon his mule and Donnie on his mule. It was some distance away from the barn, maybe two miles. The mules walked over terraces, across ditches then crossed a field called a new ground that had been a wooded area but most of the trees had been cut down, some stumps were left to be dug up in the field. Lepolion and Donnie had reached that field when for some reason Donnie's mule stumbled, Donnie fell off of the mule's back and the mule started to run. Donnie's foot got caught in a part of the bridle, the mule never stopped running until he got to the barn. Lepolion tried to catch him, but could not. We were all home waiting for the two of them to join us for dinner, instead Lepolion ran into the kitchen and told Mama and Papa that Donnie had been hurt. All of us ran to the barn as fast as we could. Mama was crying and asking Lepolion over and over is he hurt bad? I only remember his answer being that he fell off of the mule's back.

When we got to the barn someone had put Donnie in the trunk of Mrs. Avery's car. She said "I will carry him to the doctor for you". Mama and Papa got into the front seat with her. My brother Barney rode in the trunk with Donnie to hold his head. The trip to the doctor was about fifteen miles away. He was not moving or making any sound, the rest of us went back home to wait. No one ate dinner that day, we just waited. Only Lepolion knew really what had happened to him, only Lepolion saw the mule dragging him. He said over and over that he tried to catch him but could not run as fast as the mule.

When Papa, Mama and Barney came home, neither of them was saying anything. We knew Donnie was dead. Mama did not seem like herself at all, she was so upset and grief stricken. Papa tried everything he knew how to comfort her, but could not he was so worried about her because she could not be comforted. She wanted God to let her die and for him to let Donnie live.

My siblings that lived in West Virginia came home to his funeral. Theodore, Arthur, Guy, Booker and Lillie all came except Taft, he did not come. I never knew why. I try at times to remember his funeral, but for some reason I can not remember anything about it. I do remember that I thought Mama would never be the same again.

She got sick soon after my brother's death and Papa carried her to a doctor. When they came home she told us that she was going to have to eat different, because her blood pressure was too high that it could affect her heart. I was eleven when Donnie was killed. I only remember Mama being sick one time before that year. But after that she was always sick. She soon started having chest pains. Her doctor told her that her heart was getting weak and that she needed to stop working in the fields. That happened in 1940 and Donnie was fifteen years old that year.

After we gathered the crop we gave one half of everything we grew to Mr. Avery, because that was the 'sharecropping' arrangement. We went there with nothing of our own. So the agreement with him was to work for him and give him half of what we grew. Soon, Papa found a farm at another place, closer to Roanoke, Alabama and rented it. This farm was to be worked the same as before, we still did not own any farm animals, a wagon or anything that enabled us to work any other way. Again we moved in the wintertime. We moved all of our furniture on a wagon, just as we had done before. Barney was living in Roanoke at this time, because he worked there.

Barney came home when he could. One of those times when he came for the weekend, just out of the blue, no one asked him anything but he told us that Donnie did not die after they got him to the doctor's office. As the doctor had said, he told us I knew I was holding his head and I know when he stopped breathing and that was long before we got to the doctor. He no doubt lived that experience many times. Maybe that is why he decided to tell us, possibly hoping he could stop remembering it, if he talked about it.

We continued to attend the same school until that term ended. To do so we had to walk about three miles to get the bus that would take us back to Five Points School. By this time, a few buses were provided for black children.

Lepolion and Oliver got jobs at a lumber yard in Roanoke, and did not attend school anymore. When they could, they continued to help Papa do the plowing of the fields.

We all missed Donnie so much when we were in the fields working. If Mama and Papa were with us we never mentioned him, but if they were not, we talked about things he used to do or say. Just the mention of his name in Mama's presence upset her so much. Mama kept the clothes that he was wearing when he was killed as long as she lived.

When she sometimes opened the drawer where the clothes were kept, even years afterward, she would just stand looking at them crying. Mama died in 1950 of a massive heart attack, only ten years after Donnie was killed.

After moving to a different house and farm, my brothers Oliver and Lepolion even before moving they had started finding jobs to do away from home when the two of them were not needed to help on the farm. At the end of 1941, after working for a while on these jobs at a Planning Mill, they decided to buy a car. The car that they bought was a Model-A Ford.

Before getting that car they needed some kind of transportation to get to and from their jobs. These jobs were not close to our house but near Roanoke, Alabama. So they bought themselves each bicycles, before they bought the car. Gertrude and I could only ride their bikes on the weekends or when they did not need them. After getting the car they gave us the bikes.

We were two happy girls. We rode them early in the morning and late in the afternoon, anytime that we didn't have work to do. Lepolion taught Gertrude and I to drive their car. Since I was only about twelve years of age and Gertrude only fourteen, we only drove the car on field roads or roads that were made by saw millers.

Papa had never owned a car, so they taught him to drive the car. Before going into the armed services, they exchanged the Model-A ford car for a 1936 Ford. Soon after buying it they were drafted. They gave the car to Papa. After getting the car we no longer went places like to the church or into Roanoke on the wagon pulled by the mules. Mama never wanted to learn to drive and was always afraid when riding if Papa was driving. She would say to him every time "Lessie you drive too fast, you are going to cause me to have a heart attack".

When Lepolion went into the Army, the military sent Papa and Mama an allotment check. They did so because Lepolion was still living at home and helping work on the farm at the time of being drafted, so the allotment was to compensate Papa and Mama for taking him away.

When Oliver went into the Marines, Papa and Mama also received an allotment. That money was such a help to us, it made it possible for Papa to buy some farm tools he needed and two mules and a wagon.

The allotments were small. I remember one was $37 a month but in the 1940's that amount of money bought much more than it will now. Oliver got married while he was still in the Marines, so the allotment stopped from him. It was sent then to his wife. The allotment from Lepolion continued until we moved to the farm that Papa and Mama bought.

The very first year that we attended Five Points School, the school caught fire and burned to the ground. Afterward, we went to school in churches. When the school burned, no one had gotten to school that day. No one was hurt or burned. That school was much larger than the first school that I attended and had more teachers. Wood heaters were used to warm the building. If the heaters caused the fire or some other reason, I do not remember.

In 1942 Gertrude and I began attending Randolph County Training School in Roanoke. In that county, schools for black children began in July and closed in the middle of August. Schools began again in October. This schedule was arranged so that we would be home to help pick cotton.

Picking cotton was really hard work. We all had cotton picking sacks that were made to hang across our shoulders and down our sides. As we picked the cotton, we got a hand full and put it in the sacks. When the sacks got full we emptied the cotton into a basket that Papa had made. This work after a few hours became very painful. Carrying a heavy sack of cotton bend over to reach the cotton boles made everyone's back ache. If the weather got cold before we finished picking, our fingers go sore, because by then the boles have dried and are hard and sticky making it difficult to pull the cotton out. Near the end of 1942, Papa and Mama began looking for a farm to buy. By the first of 1943 they had the money to make a down payment on a farm. At this time, only Gertrude and I were the only ones of the fourteen children living at home. All that was needed was a few hundred dollars for the payment and we were so happy that they had it. The balance due on the farm was to be paid over a period of seven years.

Teen and Young Adult Years

After we moved to our farm we no longer had to walk so far to get to school each day. A bus came to within on half mile of our house. I was happy about that. The bus had no heater. We were colder once we got to school than when we got on the bus.

We walked up the road from our house, one half mile to catch the bus. Standing by the road waiting for the bus the sun kept us warm if it was not raining. Still I was happy that we now had a bus to ride. Before the bus was provided for us, it took us about one hour or longer to get to school and if it was a rainy day we were soaking wet and cold when we got to school.

Papa and Mama worked so hard after we moved to our own place. They had no help now except Gertrude and me. My brothers were all gone away from home by this time. Papa and Mama were determined to pay for the farm and not loose it. They continued to plant cotton, corn, potatoes, peanuts, sugar cane for syrup. They planted fruit trees, a big vegetable garden. We raised hogs, cows and chickens. At the end of each year a payment was due on the farm.

Making the down payment on the farm, and moving into the house required all the money my parents had at the time. They turned to Lillie and her husband for help. They lived in West Virginia, where, Thomas, Lillie's husband, worked in one of the coal mines. They gave my parents a loan. That money was needed to buy fertilizer, seeds and other supplies that were necessary to start the first crop at the new farm.

Our school started every year about the same time of the fall season that the cotton started to open and was ready to be picked. That meant Gertrude and I could not go to school until it had been in session for almost two months. I don't remember having too much of a problem catching up. Both Papa and Mama were getting older and their health was not good, especially Mama's. The potatoes had to be dug and stored away so they would not freeze in the winter months when the weather got cold. The peanuts had to be pulled up, washed and laid out to dry and then put away in bags. The vegetable s had been gathered during the summer, canned and put away. The fruit had been preserved some of it dried and put away before school started.

My first year at Randolph County Training School was summer school which was arranged for us from the middle of July until the end of August. By the end of 1943 and 1944 school year the summer school had been discontinued. I felt sorrow every month when the report card was delivered because of the number of absent days on it. We were able to gather the corn on Saturdays so we didn't have to miss so much school.

During the summer months, white ladies asked Mama if I could come to their houses and do cleaning and baby sit for them. Mama always said that I couldn't do the work good enough to work for them. Her real reason was that she did not think that I would be safe in the homes of white people without her with me. Mama asked the ladies to bring their dirty clothes to our house and she would help us wash and iron them and that is just that they did. That was called "taking in washing". Early every morning we got all the water drawn put in the pots and tubs, got the clothes and started boiling in the pot. When we came home from the fields for our middle of the day dinner, we rinsed the clothes and hung them on the lines to dry. We then went back to the field to finish our work.

Early in the next morning, we started getting the ironing done. We ironed every piece that we washed: underwear, towels, sheets, pillowcases, dresses, pants and shirts. Mama inspected every piece to make sure that each piece was ironed really well. We were paid two or three dollars for each family's wash that we completed. Together, Gertrude and I earned around eight dollars a week.

At the end of the summer, we could no longer take in washing. We saved the money we earned while we could. Once school started back, we did not have enough time at home to do the washings.

With the money that we had saved, Mama and Papa carried us to one of the fabric stores in Roanoke and we bought material for dresses, skirts, and blouses. Then we went to one of the shoe stores to buy shoes and socks that we would wear to school. After we finished picking our cotton, we sometimes picked for other people. Papa and Mama went along with us. We never went along to other people's fields. The fields were far from anyone's home to far for two girls to go alone. We could have encountered trouble from someone. Our parents tried always to protect us.

The first year that I attended Randolph County Training school the school caught fire and burned to the ground. Just as we had to do when the school burned in Five Points, we had to go to school in the different churches. There were not enough churches for all of us. Some barracks were used along with the churches. At one time that had been a CCC (Civilian Conservation Camp) at Roanoke but it had closed down by this time. CCC was a public work relief program for unemployed men that were part of the New Deal legislation signed by President Franklin D. Roosevelt. The barracks that were used were part of the camps. Those barracks were long buildings, much like army camps.

Once my classmates learned that my last school had also burned, they asked me to please do not change schools again.

During the vegetable season, almost every Saturday morning we gathered vegetables from our garden. Some of the vegetable that we did not need for our own use were put aside to sell as well as the milk and butter that was not needed at home. We got it all ready and carried it to Roanoke and sold it to different families. The day before we churned the mile to make butter and buttermilk, none of our customers wanted whole milk they all asked for buttermilk. We didn't own a refrigerator; the night before going into Roanoke with this food we used water drawn from the well to put the food in tubs. The milk and butter was put in containers and put in water. The next morning the milk and butter was as cold as the water was. The places in town that we sold this food were of course the black people side of town, place called Hill City and New Town.

At times when we went into town, Mama and I went into one store that had the nicer clothes in it. When getting inside, she asked the owner if she could take one or two of the dresses down from the place they were hanging not because she wanted to buy one but she wanted to get a good look at the seams and the way the hems were finished off and the buttonholes. She always used a pattern when sewing our clothes but the ready made ones gave her new ideas as to how to make our thing look as ready made as she could.

Before going into town, although Mama was always clean, she put on one of the prettiest dresses she had made for herself that was ironed as smooth as could be. If she was carrying me with her, she would say, "Grace we are going into the nice stores, so we must be as clean as can be. Then the white people won't object to us touching the clothes there". And they never did. It seems that we always heard from both Papa and Mama the words, clean yourselves up, and stay clean, if you are not doing dirty work there is no need to be dirty"

When I was younger, I remember asking my parents why don't colored people live in big white pretty houses and have cars to ride in. Papa always spoke right up to me and said, "Grace this is a white man's world and that is why". He also said to me "you see colored folks always work for the white people, never the other way around". I did not understand what he meant. My parent never complained about all of the hard work that they had to do. They knew it had to be done for us to survive so they did it.

Roanoke in the 1940's looked much as it does today, a small town with old buildings. At that time it was such a pretty place to me especially at night. Lights were everywhere except at our house. We did not have electricity in our house until 1947, so to go from our country home into town at night seemed very pretty to me. One of the stores we went to was named Stanback. The store Papa went to buy farm supplies was named McMurray's.

What gave me the most joy about going to Roanoke was the Martin Theater. After we carried all of our customers their milk, butter, vegetables and fruit we went into town with our parents when they had shopping to do at the dry goods store.

After we moved to our farm, no peddlers came by our house. At the dry goods store, Mama bought the thread, bias tape, laces and other notions she needed for sewing. She bought thread for sewing because she could not use the thread pulled from the fertilizer sacks like she did when I was younger on the sewing machine. After finishing with their business at the stores, they went down to Thompson's Funeral Home. In the same building the two Mr. Thompson's who where brothers operated a barber shop. There Mama and Papa waited there for me every Saturday to go to the martin Theater. There I saw a double feature plus a continuing movie. Sometimes they were questioned about sitting so long. Their answer was that their daughter needed some enjoyment in her life because she works hard all week right along with us.

Some of the money earned from the milk, butter and vegetables my parents used to buy gas for our car pay insurance premiums and to pay the electric bill after we got electricity in our house.

Many years later, one of my brothers made the comment that farming wasn't hard work. At that instant, I could almost see Papa walking behind a mule plowing the fields; bend over because of the arthritis pains in his back was so bad but still having to do that kind of work. At that time I wanted to cry for Papa, even though at the time Papa had been dead for more than twenty years. Yes, farming is hard work even for a young man.

Many years after working so hard in the fields to get the crops planted, the rain would not come when needed so the cotton and corn would not produce as we hoped it would and that was so necessary for us. Then there was the other extreme. The next year too much rain would come and that hindered the crops from producing as we hoped it would. You could say farming was like gambling. We did the work, prepared the ground, putting the seeds and plants down and hope and pray that the weather would be suitable that year. Many time if the crop did produce well then the price of cotton would fall so low that it was almost like giving it away to sale it and we still had our expenses to pay.

Getting the cotton and other seeds planted required lot of work for the four of us. A planter was needed to put down some of the seeds. Gertrude and I walked in laid off rows and dropped the seeds with our hands. A part of his seed planter Papa made in his blacksmith ship. Another instrument he made there was his fertilizer distributor. After all of my brothers left home, Mama, Gertrude and I had to help Papa do many jobs that we had never done before. When it was time to do the planting, all of the tools were put on the wagon and Papa hitched the mules to it. We climbed on the wagon with Papa and went to the field to get the planting done. One mule he fastened to the planter with seeds in it, the other mule he fastened to the fertilizer distributor. Papa always operated or walked along behind the mule and distributor holding it up as it put down the fertilizer. Gertrude and I took turns walking along behind the other mule that was pulling the planter in the rows to hold it up as it put down seeds. Mama helped by putting seeds in the planter when needed. At about ten o'clock in the morning, Mama left the field to go home to cook our dinner.

After we worked so hard getting the crops planted and gathered, my siblings remembered how good the potatoes and peanuts taste just out of the ground they wrote to us to send some to them in West Virginia. There were so many mountains in West Virginia that there was no place to plant anything. They said if we plant here, first we should have to dig down one side of a mountain. Rather than dig down one side of the mountain, they asked our parents to send some food to them. I do not remember anyone offering to come and help us in the fields. Boxes were packed with peanuts and potatoes to be sent to them.

When the potatoes were ready to be dug up, Papa hitched the mules to the wagon, put his plow, sacks and baskets on the wagon. Mama, Gertrude and I climbed on board the wagon and we went to the potato patch. Papa using the plow pulled by one of his mules began rolling potatoes out of the ground. Using the sacks and baskets, we three helpers put all of the potatoes on the wagon and brought them home.

Papa built what he called a potato hills close to our house to store them in. That was a job that I was never a helper of. They were all put in those hills, except the ones to be sent to West Virginia. The potato hills were built out of corn stalks, pine needles and dirt. First of all he laid some cornstalk flat on the ground then pine needles were laid on top of them the potatoes were placed on the pine needles and piled as high as he could without rolling down the hill. More cornstalks were laid against them to cover the potatoes completely. Then more pine needles all that were covered with dirt about four or five inches. That was done to keep the cold from causing the potatoes to freeze and ruin when the temperature went below freezing. I was never asked to help store the potatoes away; I did not know how Papa did that. My brother Oliver and his wife Opal came for visit some months ago and while he was there he helped Papa gather what was needed to put the potatoes in their winter storage. He told me that when he was a little boy he always followed Papa everywhere as much as he could and that Papa let him help.

Four of my brothers left home in the early 1930's. If they had stayed all they could have done was to farm someone else's land or work for wages, and live in poverty. One of these brothers, Taft, left home before I was born. He went to West Virginia and found work there in a coal mine. Many years passed before Taft came home again. When I saw him for the first time, I was six or seven years old. When he came home, he brought his wife and two children. I never saw Taft again alive. When I did see him for the second time he was dead. He had been shot to death by someone in West Virginia in 1945. He was the father of five children and was brought back home to be buried in Alabama.

The brother that brought back my earliest memories was Guy. He went away in the early 1930's. When Guy and his wife Irene left, they had two little boys. He also got a job in one of the coal mines. He worked where coal was dug out of the ground which was deep under the ground. The grounds caved in while he was working and Guy died by being crushed as a result of it. By that time he was the father of seven children. Guy was also brought back home to Alabama to be buried. My parents were upset and hurt for the children left behind from Taft and Guy. Papa and Mama had always worried about so many of their sons working under the ground, as they called working in the mines. They understood why they did dangerous work, to provide better living conditions for their families.

In late October every year, a fair came to town, known better now as a 'carnival'. That was a special time for me. I began thinking about and preparing for it weeks before it came. We worked hard to get all of our cotton picked. Then we hired ourselves out to earn some money. Our jobs were helping other people pick their cotton.

In those times we were paid only fifty cents for every one hundred pounds of cotton that we picked. When I first began picking for others, I could not pick a hundred pounds of cotton in a whole day but by the time the fair got to town, I had picked enough cotton to have saved three or four dollars for myself. That was enough to pay for my rides and I could buy cotton candy, hotdogs and a drink as well. On Children's Day, the admission ticket to go on the rides, into the side show and see different animals in the little zoo like area was only fifteen cents each. That day was only for school children. I remember going to the fair only once from school. The bus that I rode to school had two routes to cover so the driver told us if you leave school and go to the fair your parents will have to get you and carry you home.

When I became a teenager and had a boyfriend I made plans to see him at the fair, and it was fun for me. When we went on the rides or got to see a side show he bought both tickets. If he won prizes at the fair, he always gave them to me. The girls that danced and sang in the shows wore pretty outfits to me. As I watched the girls dance I wondered if they earned a lot of money. I was sure that they earned more dancing and singing than I did picking cotton. The work they did I was sure was not for me because I knew I could never dance the way they did.

My sister Lillie got married when I was just six years old and we have not lived in the same state since then. Sometimes when we talk about our parents and living at home with them it seems as if we grew up with different parents and in different households. I can understand why it seems that way. Lilllie did not have to work at home as I did. When she left home Mama and Papa were still young and in good health. By the time I became a teenager I had no brothers at home to help work in the fields, that meant Gertrude and I had to work like little beavers to help Mama and Papa get everything done and by this time Mama's health was really bad. When I told Lillie how hard it was for us at times, she couldn't imagine it. Even though our parents were getting old and not in good health, yet she could not see why making a living was hard for them. My older siblings did not seem to ever realize that Papa and Mama were growing old.

Near the end of the school year of 1945, Gertrude left home to go and catch the bus for school but when she got to school she did not go inside for classes, instead she had decided to get married that day. Her boyfriend picked her up soon after she got off of the bus. They left in his car, went to a justice of the peace and got married that day. Gertrude was only seventeen years old. Now with Gertrude gone, Papa and Mama and I were the only ones left to do the work. By working even harder we got it all done but not with out it taking its toll on Mama. She continued to have problems with her blood pressure and she was always tired.

Mama was not only tired from the work that she and Papa did to provide necessary provisions for us, but form the physical pains as a result of a blood pressure and heart problems. Along with the field work and the work at home, Mama and Papa took cared of some of the grandchildren that put extra work on both of them, since they were only babies to four years old. It was necessary for them to take quilts and sheets with them to make beds for them in the field. The beds had to be made up from the ground on the wagon so ants or any kind of bugs could not get on them while they slept.

Thinking about the extra responsibility for them make me feel sad. They had grief and worried over the tragic deaths of their sons. Mama and Papa always had each other to depend on during that time. I am sure that helped them to endure the hard life as long as they did.

The Pedal Type Sewing Machine

Mama always sewed our clothes. The dresses she made for Gertrude and me always most of the time were made from the same color of fabric. Other times she used fabric with same designs but was a different color. She even used the same patterns; she did that so that neither of us could say that one dress was prettier than the other. Some of the fabric that Mama used to sew garments for us was bought from the peddler.

The socks and ribbons for our hair she bought for us were alike. People many times asked if we were twins. I was two years younger than Gertrude, but as long as I can remember I was as tall or taller and always heavier than she was.

The truck that the peddler used was a regular truck. On the back part was something like a house. Inside of the house, shelves were added to all of the walls. All of his goods were kept on those shelves, going inside all of his goods were visible to see. Once each week this man came to our neighborhood in what we called the rolling store. He had on that truck most everything that country people needed like soaps, salt, soda, baking powder, canned goods, fruits, candies and gum that children like me were always happy just to see. If Mama had a little extra money, she bought us candy. Mama's little money came from sewing for someone mostly white ladies.

By the time that Gertrude and I had reached maybe ten or twelve years old, Gertrude began to help Mama to lay our patterns on the material, or sew on buttons or do some basting stitching for Mama. But sewing did not interest me at all.

The only time I stayed in the room was to be measured, to see if the pattern fit me. At times if Mama was doing sewing that required just straight stitching, she asked me to pedal the machine for her. That allowed her legs to get some rest. She always had so much to do.

When Gertrude got married she had become an excellent seamstress. I did not learn to sew until after I got married, by that time Mama had already died. I did not want to sew until my daughter was born, then I wanted to sew for her the way Mama had always done for me. I had to teach myself and was determined to do it.

When Mama sewed, she many times added lace, rickrack or embroidered some flowers, birds or other embellishment. She said that was the make the garment look store bought instead of homemade as they were. I wrote this poem to describe Mama's work:

Feather Pillows

Today I am remembering some of the jobs that Mama used to do.

She would always be creating or making something new.

One day I asked her "Mama what will that you are making be."

Is it perhaps something you are making for little me?

She told me this time, "Sorry to disappoint you dear, this is going to be something for your Papa and me".

I could hardly wait to see what it would be. Then she pulled out a bag that had been stored away, and then I knew right away what it was going to be.

There is this box now in my closet that I keep stored away. It is those feather pillows that Mama was making that day.

When Mama killed a chicken from our yard for breakfast or dinner, she saved the chickens feathers to use in pillows and she saved enough at one time to make a feather mattress for her and Papa's bed. When I think about all the different items that were made on the pedal-type sewing machine, it is not easy to picture all of that work as being accomplished manually.

My mother began working as a mid-wife when I was a little girl, maybe before then, but I was little when I remembered first about it. I never wanted Mama to go away from the home and leave me. When different men came to our house to get her to help their wives give birth to a baby, I always cried when she left as if she were never coming home again. Once she was going to help a mother deliver I decided that time I was going with her, although she did not intend to take me with her. She told me that Miss Headie would be here to help Papa take care of me while she was away. Miss Headie was a handicapped woman that had no home of her own. She lived with different families in our neighborhood. She was helpful to everyone. If a woman had a baby she moved in with that family and if someone got sick she was there to help out. She many times stayed with us for weeks at a time.

She helped Mama make quilts and helped to mend our clothes when needed. Whatever Mama had to do when she was at our house, Miss Headie was right there with her helping out. I am sure she was trusted by everyone. When Mama was called on to help some lady have her baby she knew she could count on her to help out.

As Mama got ready to leave I was determined to follow her. I remember asking her over and over again to take me with her. She looked down at me but did not say anything to me. Miss Headie closed the door when she left to keep me inside. I was going to hit her with an iron that Mama used to iron our clothes with, the kind that you put close to the fire in the fireplace to heat or put on top of the wood cooking stove to heat. I wanted to move her out of my way. Papa stopped me and took me in his lap and let me cry myself to sleep. When I woke up the next morning, Mama was home in the kitchen cooking our breakfast.

When I was about seven or eight years old, Mama came down with pneumonia. It was a really bad case. She almost did not survive it. She said after getting well while she was so sick, she thought that she heard Gertrude and me in the back of the bed singing to her. Our oldest sister Lillie had asked us to sing to Mama. Lillie came home to help out when Mama was so sick. Dr. Piper came to see her everyday. It seemed then that Lillie was always doing something for Mama, washing her, giving her medicine or changing her bed. Papa cooked for use while Mama was sick. When he was away, Lillie cooked along with taking care of Mama. This was in the summertime, because before the doctor left everyday, he told Papa or Lillie to always keep the windows raised, she needed all of the fresh air that she could get.

While Mama was so sick, Gertrude and I many times sat on the floor at the foot of Mama's bed and played with our dolls. The wind caused the curtains to move in and out the window at times and we enjoyed watching it do that. Lillie thought that our singing would help Mama, give her a reason to want to live. Our singing did just that. Because she began to remember how she had been treated after her mother died by her step mother. She said that she prayed to God and asked to let her live until her youngest child (me) was old enough to take care of herself.

Mama did get well, and it seemed in no time she was herself again, doing many things around our house.

Lillie is fourteen years older than I am. I remember only a little about her living at home. I remember her being in the kitchen helping Mama cook for us. Other times I remember her combing my hair. She wore pretty heigh-heel shoes that I liked so much. I said to myself that when I got older, I would only wear high heal shoes.

The cleaning of our yards was a job that can easily be described as hard manual labor. This cleaning was always done on Saturdays. Grass was not left in our yard to grow or any around the flower beds. The grass that grew, we used our hoes too chopped it down and we used our brooms to clean the other trash in the yard. It was swept away in a pile and when it dried, was set on fire.

Our brooms for sweeping the outside were made from dogwood tree limbs that we went into the woods and gathered. Those limbs were stripped clean of some of the leaves. That par t of the limb or limbs we tied together with strings in three or four places depending on the length of the limbs. They were then ready to begin working with. Stooping over to sweep with those brooms was harder work than using our hoes to chop weeds from around the cotton.

What was the most difficult about that work of cleaning the yards was going under our house to sweep there. We put pads on our knees to do that because that sweeping was done while crawling on the ground. That mad our knees, backs, necks and arms hurt. It was so dusty under the house. As soon as the sweeping was finished, we all had to take off our clothes and take a bath. We were too dusty to sit anyplace in our house. Then there was big pile of dirty clothes to be washed.

Every feature of laundering was hard work. First gallons and gallons of water had to drawn up from our well and then put into two iron wash pots. Wood was gathered and a fire was made under the wash pots. When the water got hot in the pots some was dipped out and added to the water that had been put in tubs to make it warm. There the clothes got the first of the washing then they were put into pots where the fires were burning. The clothes were put in these pots for thirty minutes to an hour depending on how dirty they were. The soap was homemade by Mama.

To make the soap, grease form cooking meats were saved also skins from hogs flesh and small amount of water was put in one of the iron wash pots, when not being used to wash our clothes and other washables. Mama added the meat skins the meat drippings and a box of lye, sometimes called potash. She let that all boil in the iron pot until it became a thick mass. She then raked the fire from under the pot; then as it cooled it became solid. It was taken out of the pot, cut in pieces and we used it to clean the things that had to be washed.

When the fertilizer sacks were cleaned, mama made spreads for our beds from some of them. The sacks were taken to the pedal type sewing machine, and then sewn together.

My Parents – Mollie and Lessie Smedley ca. 1947

Mama wanted some beauty for our house. She put a solution of some color of dye in the wash pot after we had pulled small sections of the material, tied them with some of the strings that was taken from the sacks when we opened them up. They were put in the hot solution of dye. Mama followed the instructions on the dye package took the material out, rinsed it and let them dry on the clothes line.

We then cut the strings that were holding the sections. The designs that formed form the tied strings had jagged white circles all over the material. Mama, Gertrude and I then pulled at the edges of the material. We pulled out strings for about four inches to make fringes around all sides except the top. The top side was hemmed. Mama then made starch from some of the flour she used to cook with and put the bed spread in it. She let it dry until it was still left a little damp and them we ironed it until not one wrinkle was left.

Mama embroidered flower or some other design on the curtains she made to match the color that she put on the bed spread. There was never an end to our work. Mama said that no one was going to give us the things that we needed so we much do for ourselves.

I enjoyed looking at the different home shows on the television. If Mama were living at this time, she would be as interested to watch, create, invent or originate items or prepare food as any of them.

Today when I decide to make an outfit for myself or curtains for my windows, a quilt, a comforter, pillow cases, pillow shames or bed skirts or upholsterer a chair or cover some cushions, I will go to the nearest fabric shop and select the fabric. I will buy one kind for the garment, another kind for the curtains, another kind of fabric designed especially for upholstering. I will select lace, fringe, welting cord and other notions I will need. That would not be true for Mama. To do much of her sewing, first she had to wait for fertilizer to be used from the sacks. She then washed them to remove all of the letters and numbers on the sacks that sometimes were so hard to fade away. We boiled them in the wash pot, and scrubbed them on a rub board. We then beat them on a block with a stick, and then they were left hanging on the clothesline in the sun for days. That was done to make the sacks as white as possible.

The strings holding the sacks together had to be unraveled and saved. Mama used those strings for thread to do many jobs. When she wanted to make a table cloth and to have a fringe on the edge, she created her own fringe. She studied the directions of the weave on the sack and then pulled strings out across the grain that made the end of the fabric into a fringe.

When Mama put lace on a pair of pillow cases, she used some of the thread that was raveled from the sacks as crocheting thread. She then crocheted pretty lace for pillow cases.

Graduation

For me, finishing high school and then going away to college was a hope and dream that I had for years. I wanted to teach children who were just beginning to attend school. I decided for many reasons that to get married anytime soon was not a wise thing to do. I had in mind working, living at home if possible and buying some things that would make Papa and Mama's work a little easier for them. They needed a pump for the well that would eliminate the burden of having to draw the water up from the well and carry it in buckets and tubs to wherever it was needed.

In 1947 we finally got electricity in our house. By my graduation in 1949 we still did not own a refrigerator. Mama needed one for many reasons. We had to milk the cow twice a day, when the weather was hot to prevent the milk from spoiling. We drew water from the well into which we would pour the fresh milk. After milking the cows, and getting water from the well that was needed for use in the kitchen, for taking baths, and for drinking, then one of us put a jar of milk into the bucket that was used to draw water out of the well. The bucket was then lowered into the well carefully. When the bucket reached the water in the well, it filled the bucket with water and was left there all night. The next morning, when the bucket was drawn up, the milk was really cold. Some of the milk was left out, and placed into a five gallon churn to clabber. Only then could we make butter from it, and also have buttermilk to drink.

More than anything else, I wanted to get my parents a washing machine. All of my life Mama had to do washing the hard way. I felt that if I could change that for her , it would give her so much joy and end that part of her laboring. It would not end the entire burden of the hard work for her and Papa because they still had to farm to provide for themselves.

I never had a dress that was bought ready made until I finished high school. From the time I was a young teenager I had wanted a black dress. When I asked mama to buy black fabric she always said to me "Grace you do not want a black dress". So she never made me one. Now that I was about to graduate from high school, Mama took me to Roanoke to buy me a ready made dress for my graduation. She also allowed me to select the dress. I saw a black one and thought that it was just what I had always wanted. Again, Mama didn't want me to get a black dress but she let me have it anyway. Maybe she thought if she did not let her have this black one, I just might have to bury her. I had seen the pretty black dresses that Mama made for the white ladies, some was black velvet suits and to me they were so pretty. She made dresses in other colors but for some reason the black ones were the prettiest to me. Mama made black dresses for herself also and told me black dresses are for older ladies not young girls. That did not stop me from wanting one for myself. I wore that black dress to my graduation. All of my classmates had on pretty pastel color dresses. Now I knew at last that Mama was right. I did not want a black dress. After that day I never wore that dress again.

I went to the prom when I was in the eleventh grade and Mama made me a beautiful white satin dress that I loved so much. My classmates could not believe that my Mama had made it. After wearing it to the prom, she shortened it so that I could wear it to other events.

The dress that I had for my senior prom that year was made over for me. My Aunt Hattie had sent us a box that spring as she had done so many times before. In that box was this long blue formal dress that she was going to completely change the style and she did. The dress was made of blue satin and yards and yards of blue netting over it. Mama used only a small amount of netting, eliminating the sleeves completely. The wide ruffle on the bottom was removed. I came to realize watching her alter and redesign that dress that to make one from scratch seemed to be much easier. Although at that time I had never made a dress for myself.

When prom night came, Mama did all she could to help me get dressed from holding the mirror for me to see my hair in the back and how the dress looked from the back, to rubbing the lotion on my arms for me. Thinking about it now, if I had asked her to help me take a bath, she would have no doubt gladly done it for me. When my date, long time boyfriend, and future husband, Guy Marable, came to get me to take me to the prom he said that I looked really nice. I felt better about the dress. I had not complained to Mama about it. I knew she had done the best that she could for me, but I did so much want a dress made from new material but after buying the black dress for me she could not afford it.

I was so happy that I had finished high school but knowing that my forty-five classmates and I would go our separate ways made me sad. Some of the young men I did not see again for over forty years. More than half of them I never saw again. Some went into the armed services and soon afterward were sent to Korea. Some of the girls were able to get into college. Others went to states in the North like Ohio and Michigan. Their desire was to find good—paying jobs in those states that were not available in Alabama at the time.

Mama asked my brothers since they were all away working if they would help me get started going to college. Mama and Papa could not help me, and I knew that well. Mama's health was continuing to get worse. All of my brothers had families and could not help me at all. Having families was not the only reason they gave for not helping me to continue my education. They felt that I would not complete the schooling because they felt that I would marry the first man that asked me. I never understood why my siblings thought I would not be able to choose the right man to spend the rest of my life with.

I would have liked to have gone from high school to college. That is what I wanted to do so much but instead of doing that I went to the fields to help Papa and Mama get the crops planted. Cotton, corn, peanuts, white and sweet potatoes were all planted. I turned to my siblings again. I thought if I could go and stay with one of them until I got a job, I could work and send myself to college. Again the answer was no. I started to believe that I would never land a job and get myself in the position to help my parents. Working in the fields with them was a help but it did not provide me with an income. Hopefully at the end of the year a little money would be made after selling the cotton, but instead, all the money was needed to make the payment on the farm and to pay other bills.

Contents of My Class Autograph Book

Names of some of my favorite teachers:
Miss Miles
Miss Chatman
Mr. Higgins
Miss Abraham
Mrs. Cole
Miss Riley
Miss Rowe
Miss Cartee
Mrs. King

My favorite sports:
Basketball and Baseball

Chums:
Johnny Whittaker
James Watts

Clyde Holly
Pearlie Treadwell
Eva Billingsly
Beatrice Harris
Drucellia Pallard
Martha
Kit
Maggie
Mary Anderson
Holston Longshore

Commencement Date May 20, 1949
Autographs
For Lo! The winter is past. The rain is over and gone. The flowers appear on the earth. The time of the singing of birds is come. The voice of turtle dove is heard in our land and now is your time.
Signed Mother, Song of Solomon 2:11,12

Dearest Grace,
It has been great knowing you and being a friend of yours these few years. Now that we are about to part, remember our class motto. "The past forever gone, the futures still our own".
A pal,
Beatrice

Dear Grace
It has been enjoyable knowing you as a friend, and to know you have been one of the most dignified seniors of the senior's class. Someday I hope to be in your foot steps. So keep climbing someday the goal will be yours.
A very true schoolmate, Velma Carter

Hello Grace
It has been very nice knowing you these few years and it will be very lonesome to depart. Remember our class motto: "The past forever gone, the futures still our own."

Signed a classmate
Ruby L. Molden

Dear Grace
It has been swell knowing you these years. Remember our class motto: "The past forever gone, the futures still our own."
A classmate
Marie Johnson

Dearest Grace
When everyone has forsaken you, you can be sure of this one who will always care.
Always Frank

Dear Grace
Time has come for us to part, being a classmate with you was enjoyable, the future is your success and I hope you make the best of life.
A pal
Clyde

Hi Grace
Life has been wonderful knowing you these few years. Now we are fading away to a different land out in the world. I hope you much happiness.
Classmate
Clinton Scales

Dearest Grace
Anything worth doing is worth doing well.
A classmate
Fannie B. Barsh

Dear Grace
Life has been nice knowing you these few years. I have always known you as a friend. Continue and you'll be sure to make a great woman

some day. Our motto: the past forever gone, the futures still our own.
Your friend
Maudie Reynolds

Dear Grace
Grace you have been a very nice girl and always thinking of me who love to have fun at all times. (Smile)
J.H. (Whit) Whittaker

Dear Grace
The rose may whiter, the flowers may die, the world may forget you but never will I.
Classmate Adella Scales

Dear Grace
When you are gone away I'll wait until the day for your return. Remember your class motto "The past forever gone, the futures still our own".
Your Devoted Friend
Guy Marable

Dear Grace
It has been nice knowing you these long years. Now we are about to part. Make the best of our life.
A friend
James

Hello Grace
I had a very nice time in school with you. Grace I wish you the very happy life and success.
Yours Truly
Holston Longshore

Dear Grace
Life was fun in the beginning, but now we must part.

Classmate
Lorina Bell

Dear Grace
Please don't forget the day you first met Guy because he gave you a good time.
B.L. Anderson
P.S. Don't forget to write

Hello Grace
The only way to get to the top of a hill is to start at the bottom.
A friend
Horace

Dear Grace
It has been most enjoyable working with you this school term. It is my wish that the greatest success will be yours.
Sincerely, B.A. Outland

Dear Grace
"Truth above all"
Classmate, Mary

Dear Grace
I've enjoyed going to school with you though these long years we were together. I found no change in you. You have always been a very nice girl. Hope your future will be a happy one.
Classmate
Pearile

Dear Grace
It has been nice knowing you these years. Please remember "a journey of a thousand miles began with one step".
A classmate
Lolita Burton (Gertrude)

Dear Grace
If you do the best when you are out in the world, do your best and the best will come back to you. Always remember me as your friend. I'll never forget you and the good times we have had at good old R.C.T.S.
Love Always, Annette

Dear Grace
I've very sorry to say we must part. You do the very best you can and the best will come back to you. I hope you all the luck in the world.
Love Elenor

Dear Grace
It has been nice knowing you as a classmate but now we must part. So I wish you all the luck, you and Guy Marable.
A pal
Charlie Hendricks

Dear Grace
It has been a pleasure knowing you these years. When you are out in the world remember "American end in I can".
A classmate
Maggie Dunson

Dear Grace
It has been very nice knowing you and being your classmate. I sincerely hope that you will continue to be a nice girl as you are now.
Always remember me as a friend
Mildred

Hello Grace
I really don't know what to say, seems all of the people have said all of the nicest things there is to be said. So I'll remind you of our

motto "The past forever gone, the future is our own". Just make the best of it.
Love
Frances Alford

Dear Grace
If at first you don't succeed try and try again.
Our classmate
George Morgan

Hello Grace
The past forever gone, the futures still our own.
Classmate
Fannie Busbee

Dear Grace
The futures still our own, the past has already gone
A friend, Howard Poole

Dear Grace
It has been indeed a pleasure knowing you these years. Remember as we are about to part, to give the world the best you have and yours shall be greater in return. Remember "don't tell all you know, but know all you tell".
A classmate
Ethel

Dear Grace
Now is about time for us to part. You have been a very nice classmate and when you go to college, I wish you much success and happiness.
Yours truly,
Wylodine Seymoor

Hello Grace

It has been a great pleasure of knowing you. As we are about to depart from school, I hope you all the luck in the world.
A friend, Eva Trammell

Dearest Grace
Now that school is our and we must part still Grace I will always hold you in my heart.
Truly your friend
Charlie E. Holiday

Dearest Grace
When your days on earth are over, and your feet no longer trod. May your name in Gold be written in the Autograph of God
A friend, Mary Sue Watson
P.S. Best wishes to you in the future. Keep climbing in through the roads may be rugged.

Dear Grace
The stairway to success can never be attained by running. Take your life seriously and tread courageously and surely and it will be attained.
A classmate
Bernice Casandra O'neal

Hello Grace
As we are, so we do. And as we do so it is done to us. Cultivate the art of conversation.
Your classmate
Bertha Mae

Dear Grace
It has been nice knowing you and I hope you much success as you go on in life.
A friend and classmate
Mildred Finch

Dear Grace

Now is almost the hour when we must say goodbye. Soon we'll be sailing far, far away from each other. Don't forget the six years we have spent together. I will see you in Ohio this summer. Write me.

Your pal

Eva

There's No Place Like Home

In August of 1949, my father's sister Aunt Ora and her husband Uncle Jesse who had lived in Birmingham as long as I could remember came for a visit one weekend. They always came to see us in the summertime. While still at our house, Aunt Ora asked me what my plans were since I had finished high school. I told her that I wanted to find work some place but had not been able to. Mama then asked her is she thought that I could find a job in Birmingham. She said yes and Mama then asked if she would let me go home with her and live with her and Uncle Jesse and work for a while there. She agreed to let me go with them. Mama and I got my clothes ready and we left that afternoon.

I still remember how much I disliked being away from home and how I missed my parents. Never before had I stayed away from home for more than one night at a time. Staying overnight with a classmate was not much fun for me. I did it at times, but was always glad to get home the next day.

I wanted to work someplace, but did not think or know about what being away from home was like. I knew the only way I would be able to go to college was to work, save my money and send myself. I found a job about two weeks after I got to Birmingham. Now to leave home suddenly, I don't think I expected life to be the same. I was there to work, to earn money for myself and not to be Aunt Ora's and Uncle Jess' little girl. Knowing myself, I did not want to be mothered by Aunt Ora. My problem was I was not prepared for that new life. Maybe someone should have told me that this is no place like home. I soon learned that was why I was so miserable. I probably could have made living away from home a little easier for myself if I had been a little attentive with Aunt Ora. I could have knocked on her bedroom door at night, told her goodnight and from time to time, thanked her for letting me live with her, but I never did any of those things.

The only jobs available for black girls were domestic work. My first job was working for Dr. and Mrs. Williamson. When getting to work in the morning, I cleaned the kitchen, then made all of the beds, cleaned four bathrooms, vacuumed the floors and polished or dusted the furniture. Most of this I did every day that I worked. Mrs. Williamson did the wash but I did the ironing. There were three children in the family and they made little messes that needed cleaning up. Although the work was different, it was not a problem, because I was used to working. I had learned at home from Mama that homes needed to be kept clean, our bodies and our clothes as well. I took care of the three year old Catherine in the afternoons. Mrs. Williamson always went out someplace at that time. I earned $5.00 a day working for that family. I worked only four days a week there. So I looked until I found someone who needed help only two days and was paid the same.

If I had done that type of work in my hometown of Roanoke, I would have earned only $1.00 a day. My bus fare to and from work was twenty cents a day and I paid Aunt Ora $5.00 a week to live with her.

Aunt Ora was not a well woman, therefore not easy to please. I never knew what I did to upset her. I went to work six days a week, came home in the afternoon. I never went anyplace else. I would have been afraid in that city to do so, since I had never been to a city before. When I asked her if I could help her cook, although I knew very little about cooking, she answered with a question, "Grace am I not cooking to please you?" And I would say that although I cannot cook as good as your Mama, I do the best I can. If I asked to let me help her do the wash, she would say that she didn't need me to help because she had a washing machine and that was something that my Mama didn't have. I only stayed five of the nine months as I had originally planned to stay with Aunt Ora that I worked in Birmingham. Mama's sister Dora lived in Birmingham also. She was disabled because of a stroke she had many years earlier. Uncle Thornton, her husband and Mrs. Fack took care of her. Mrs. Fack did not stay with her at night and Uncle Thornton worked at night so she was left alone at night. I went over from time to time to visit her. One day she asked me if I would come and live with her so at night she would not be alone. I was happy do so. I did not think I would be any more miserable there than I was at Aunt Ora's.

My boyfriend, Guy Marable came to Birmingham about once a month to visit me. When I began to feel that I could not live there any longer, that is when he came up to see me. He always carried me to someplace for dinner. It was a small restaurant, someplace downtown Birmingham that was run by some black lady. We were not allowed then to go to a really nice one. Only white people could go to those nice places.

We went to the same theaters as the white people did, but had to sit in the balcony. When a movie with black actors and actresses was shown, it was always a late show that was shown after twelve o'clock midnight. Since Guy had to drive the one hundred miles back home, we hardly ever saw a late movie. The next day Guy had to go to work with his father at his saw mill.

Sometimes when Guy came to visit me, he brought my little niece Kaye with him. Kaye had lived at home with us since she was born. She was my sister Gertrude's little girl. Seeing Kaye for a day along with Guy really gave me a lot of joy. Gertrude was never selfish about sharing Kaye with me. She loved her child and could understand how Papa, Mama and I loved her too. She was not just Gertrude's little girl but our little girl.

I saved as much of the money that I earned as I could. My plans were still to send myself to college. The college that I wanted to go was Alabama A&M. I needed only enough money for one quarter. Then I hoped to get on a five year plan where I would work at the school and attend classes.

A short while after I started to work, one of my brothers, Oliver came home for a visit. He agreed to make a down payment on a refrigerator for Mama and Papa but would not be able to make the seven dollars a month payment on it. Mama asked me if I could send her the money for the payments and I agreed to send her what she needed. My parents had been taking care of their little son that summer and that is why they came down as well to visit and pick up Todd and take him home. Almost every summer my parents would keep some of the grandchildren.

Guy and I had talked about getting married someday but I didn't want it to be anytime soon. He asked me to let him send me to college, since he knew that was what I wanted to do. My answer to him was no because I thought that was the right thing to say to him. I felt that it would obligate me to him in a way I did not want to be since I was not ready to marry him. He knew what I wanted to do for my parents, so he did not push or pressure me about anything.

I had not talked to Papa and Mama about all I wanted to do for the two of them. It was something I thought needed to be done. They were my parents who had worked so many years for us, worried about us, cried with us when we could not have something we wanted.

After working for nine months in Birmingham, I had by then saved the money that I needed for school as well as enough to give Mama three months payment on her refrigerator. I hoped that by the time that was used up that I would be working at Alabama A&M and somehow would be able to send her the money she needed each month.

I went home to spend a few days with my parents before going on to college. My first quarter there was the summer months, June, July and August. When summer school ended I went home to wait and see if I would be able to get on the five year plan.

While I was home waiting, someone told me that the Superintendent of the Randolph County schools were hiring black girls and boys that had finished the twelfth grade to teach in the black children schools in the rural areas of the county. I decided that I would try to get a job in one of the schools. The superintendent gave me a job. A high school had been built at Roanoke for black children by that time, but most of the rural county schools were in churches. These schools carried grades one through six. Their only was one teacher to teach all six grades. The one that I would work in had two teachers. I was to teach grades one, two and three. I was happy that I had a job that year but I did not start work until November. That was fine with me because I could then help Mama and Papa gather the crop.

My plans were hopefully to be able to teach every year and go to college each summer until I was able to get a degree. It seemed my hopes to help my parents were going to come true. Papa, Mama and I worked so hard that year to get all of the crops gathers. That year they would make the last payment on the farm.

By the end of October all the gathering was finished. Papa went and made the last payment on the farm. In the very next month Mama became sick. For many years, Mama had been going to a chiropractic doctor along with continuing to see a medical doctor. When I was really young, Papa started having bad stomach problems. The chiropractor was able to help him get over that condition. After that if some us kids hurt a foot or strained our back somehow, we were always taken to see the chiropractor.

When Mama got sick after Donnie died, she began seeing a chiropractor every week for a while. When she got sick in November of 1950, Papa took her to the same chiropractor. At that visit the doctor advised Papa and Mama that he was not able to help her anymore. He told Papa to take Mama to a medical doctor.

Papa took her to a medical doctor that day. As soon as he examined Mama he told Papa that he needed to keep her in the hospital and start giving her medicine for her blood pressure problem and something for the pains in her chest and stomach and that she had suffered a heart attack. The medicine that she needed for her heart was not available but he called a pharmacy in Montgomery to send the medicine that she needed. He could only give her the medicine that he had that day but as soon as the medicine was sent to him for her heart, he would give it to her. Mama didn't want to stay in the hospital and she told Papa that if he left her there that she would never spend another night at home. Papa thought that was the best thing to do for her because he knew how much pain she was experiencing. So he had her admitted to the hospital. The doctor got the medicine a few days later and started giving it to her but it never stopped her pains in her stomach and chest. Although not meaning to harm herself she wanted to live as much as anyone. Mama was only sixty two years odd at the time of her death. She prayed that she would live until her youngest child was grown. She got the answer that she wanted because I was twenty one years of age at the time of her death.

I started my job teaching the first through the third grade in a school very close to our house the same month of mama's death. Very soon afterward, Papa had a pump put in the well and he hired a lady to come to our house to wash for us every week. Gertrude and her little daughter Kaye had moved back home, but Gertrude started a job teaching in September. The job was too far away to come home every day. So, she boarded with a family who lived close to the school. She came home every Friday afternoon. Kaye never went with her to her job; she stayed home with Papa and me. Kaye was only four years old at this time.

When I began working, I carried Kaye to school with me. Papa had to work away from home at times and could not always take Kaye with him. Once she started attending school with me, she wanted to do all of the work that the other children were doing. If they read, she wanted to do it too. The writing, spelling, coloring or whatever, she would say that she could do It; and she did everything well. When school closed that spring, Kaye was doing the first grade schoolwork as well as the children who were six years old.

That winter after Mama died it was only Papa, Kaye, and I at home during the week days. We missed Mama so much. In 1949, I joined Mama in her Bible studying. The first subject that was of interest to me was the Bible's promise that the dead will live again. I had read different passages from the Bible as Mama was having her studies before, but most of the time I did not understand what I had read. This day was different. All of the different Bible texts dealt with that one subject.

I had gone to funerals, and to cemeteries, and had seen caskets lowered into the ground. In those times, everyone that attended the funeral remained at the grave site until the men began putting the dirt around the box that the casket was lowered into. That scene stuck indelibly in my mind for days afterward. I wondered then as a little girl, how a dead person can ever have life again. That day in Mama's bible study, I began to get answers to that question and others. I enjoyed living and never wanted to die, dreading the thought that I would one day.

When Mama died in 1950 I had only been studying the Bible seriously for about a year. All the reasons for death I did not fully understand, but I knew from what I had read in the bible in John 5:28-29, which says according to the New World Translation of the Holy Scriptures: "Do not marvel at this, because the hour is coming in which all those in the memorial tombs will hear his voice and come out, those who did good things to a resurrection of life, those who practiced vile things a resurrection of judgment." Another Bible account which mentions that same promise is found in Acts 24:15. According to that same Bible translation it reads: "And I have hope toward God, which hope these men themselves also entertain, that there is going to be a resurrection of both the righteous and the unrighteous." I knew that meant the coming back to life of the dead, but when and how, I did not then understand. Having that little knowledge was enough to give me some hope that death did not have to mean that the ones dead could never have life on this earth again. Still the death of a parent or of other loved ones is devastating.

When the school year 1950-1951 ended, Guy was again working in Detroit. We planned to get married in the fall of that year. That summer he asked me to come there for a couple of weeks and visit him, and that would enable me to see and learn a little about what it was like there. I agreed to go there. He sent me a round trip bus ticket. That was a little scary but exciting for me all at the same time going to a big city of Detroit, Michigan for the first time. Papa agreed to let me go visit Guy, but I could not help thinking what Mama might have said about that trip.

When I arrived in Detroit, Guy had arranged for me to stay with a cousin of his who was married to a lady that I had known all of my life. At one time she was a girlfriend of my brother Lepolion. Guy lived with his oldest sister Ruth, who had been living in Detroit for many years with her family.

My first weekend there, Guy took me to Canada. That was the first time that I had been out of the United States, and it was fun and exciting for me. Mama had enjoyed reading about far away places and perhaps she would have been happy for me to be there. On another occasion, he took me to Belle Isle in Detroit where we had lunch at a nice food stand and walked on the beach together and talked about everything. We talked about where we wanted to live after we got married, if we were going to have children and if so, how many. We also went to the Paradise Theater and see a funny comedian named Moms Mabley who became a popular star in the following years.

When my two week stay was over, Guy took me to Columbus, Ohio to visit my oldest sister Lilly for a few days. My brother Melvin came to Columbus to visit me; and from there, I went home with him to Pittsburgh, Pennsylvania, so that I could see his family. After visiting Pittsburgh, I went back to Detroit to visit Guy for a few more days before I returned to my home in Roanoke.

By the time I returned home it was nearing the time for Papa and I to start gathering in the crops. That ended up being the last year that I helped him gather his crop. In late August the cotton began to open with the boles busting open and the cotton pushing out so pretty and white. We began picking it on the first week of September. That year the cotton crop looked really good as if it would produce a bale on every acre. Both Papa and I cooked for ourselves, because many things he had to tell me how to prepare. I stayed home until the entire crop was gathered. Papa and I picked all of the cotton, with no one helping us.

When it was all finished, I boarded a bus to leave home again. This time it would not be temporary but permanent, and that was what I wanted to do. I was now ready to be a wife and to spend the rest of my life with the man that I loved. When I got to Detroit, Guy had obtained our marriage license and had rented an apartment for us. Until the weekend came for us to get married, I stayed with his sister Alice and her family in Inkster, Michigan which was about ten miles away from Detroit. We married the next weekend after I arrived on November 24, 1951.

I missed Papa so much and worried about him since he was alone now. He had begun dating Miss Syrenthea before I left home but had not yet married her. They did get married about a year after Guy and I did. I often wondered what Papa was having for dinner. He was a good cook, but I hated for him to do all his work and have to do all the cooking for himself as well. Papa had learned to cook after his mother died, and that was when he was just a young boy. Mama said that he always cooked when she had a baby, so cooking was nothing new for him. I would have to stop worrying about him and decide what to cook for my new husband and myself. I had a lot to learn about cooking. I know Guy knew more about cooking than I did. Guy was patient, never complained about anything and never said he did not like what I had prepared. He was loving and considerate at all times.

Life with Husband and Children

Six months after Guy and I were married, our plans changed as to which state we would live in. Soon after moving into our little apartment I realized that I enjoyed being domestic. The apartment that we moved into that day consisted of a bedroom, one closet and a sitting area upstairs. Our kitchen and bathroom was in the basement. We moved into our apartment on our wedding day. Before going to the apartment, we shopped for grocery and then went home, put up the grocery all of our cookware and dishes we put away and together we prepared our dinner.

Guy and I went to our living space upstairs and put away clothes, our sheets, pillow cases that we did not use that day on the bed, also the towels and wash cloths. We bought those things for ourselves a few days before the Saturday we got married. We bought a couch, chair and a lamp for the sitting area. We bought a beautiful chest of drawers and dresser for the bedroom. We did not need to buy a bed because the apartment had a bed that pulled down out of the wall, a Murphy bed.

Going away someplace that day did not cross my mind. It was my honeymoon, I was having a good time and I was happy. We started discussing and looking at new houses. Some of the houses were still under construction and others were completed and waiting for someone to buy. The houses were not in Detroit, but in Inkster, Michigan. It was so exciting, and I was so happy. To think of myself owing a house that no one had ever lived in and to have a husband that wanted me to have that. Sometimes I felt most like I was asleep and would wake up and realize it was just a dream. I had just come out of the cotton fields and from cleaning two family homes, for a few dollars a day. However, it was no dream. It was real. My husband had a job working in a foundry that paid well and he worked seven days a week on that job. He never seemed to mind going to the job every day.

As mentioned above, our plans changed when Mr. Marable, Guy's father, wrote Guy a letter and asked him if he would come back home and help his younger brothers to operate the sawmill. Mr. Marable had begun to have some health problems.

Guy told me he wanted to help out at home and asked me if I would mind moving back to Alabama. I did not mind that move back because I had no doubt about being provided for. We had been married only a short time, but I knew Guy was going home to work. He worked for his father, along with his brothers, before going to Michigan, and I knew he would continue. Guy told me before we left Michigan that he would build us a house as soon as he could. Within a few weeks after that letter came, we left the state of Michigan to return to Alabama. We moved into the house with Papa. He told us before we left Michigan that we could. He reminded us that later that year, he planned to marry Miss Syrenthia, but he was glad for us to stay with him until our house was ready.

Before Guy and I left Detroit to go back to Alabama, which was home for the both of us, Guy's sister Alice prepared for us a big box of food that we enjoyed so much. She packed fried chicken, cold potato salad, sweet potato pies, sausage and biscuits and some deviled eggs. We bought sodas and ice and put it in a cooler chest also fruit and nuts for ourselves to have to eat as we traveled home. We had not been traveling much longer than an hour when we started eating our food.

We traveled by car in those days, and it was absolutely necessary to carry your food with you. Most restaurants along the roads did not serve black people. Some of the gas station attendants even complained when they were pumping gas into our car. They said things like "How did a colored man get a car like this", and then without waiting for and answer they would ask "Did you steal it?" Those words were so humiliating to us, especially to Guy. When we were talked to that way, afterwards Guy was always very quite for a long time, feeling, I am sure, shamed and belittled, but could not say or do anything. To do so would have made matters even worse.

During the drive en route to Alabama, we could not use a rest room at any gas stations or restaurants along the way. We had to find a hidden off-road area, then drive a distance far enough to get completely out of sight of the main road, and far away from any houses to relieve ourselves. We carried in the trunk of our car, soap, and water for washing our hands and to drink. I had not travelled much by car before then, but Guy had gone to Michigan by car many times before. He knew all of the rules, all of the dos and don'ts that blacks had to observe while traveling. We did not ask anyone to sell us food or to use the restroom.

The whole trip was not all bad. Guy and I were together and I had happy hopes, thoughts of my own house which I would decorate just the way I wanted it to be. Mama was so creative and I knew I inherited some of her know-how. I surely wanted to do things and make things we needed with my own hands. Slowly but surely I did learn.

Guy began building us a house very soon after we got to Alabama. Monday through Friday, he worked at the sawmill. Some weeks, he worked on a half-day on Saturday. The rest of the weekend he worked on our house. By November of 1952, our house was completed enough to move into. Both of us were anxious and excited about moving into our new house. When Mr. Marable died that same month, it was really a shock and a surprise for me, because I did not realize he was so sick.

Our plan was not to have any children for a while, but shortly after we moved into our house in November of 1952, I became pregnant. Our little bundle of joy was born in August of 1953. She was a beautiful little girl that we named Regina Ellene. Four years later in 1957, we had a son, Stacy.

Me with husband, Guy, and daughter, Regina on her wedding day in 1977

The move from Detroit was just the beginning of the many times that we moved. After Mr. Marable died, Guy and his brothers and their mother, Mrs. Marable, worked really hard to get everything done. Mrs. Marable milked lots of cows twice everyday. She sold milk to the Carnation Company. Six of her children were still at home. Four of them were still in school. Mrs. Marable always had a big vegetable garden, that she worked in and always had plenty vegetables for them. Guy and I gathered vegetables from her garden to eat. In the spring of 1953, Guy and I began planting our own garden. The first garden that we planted produced for us a lot of vegetables. We planted white potatoes, sweet potatoes, turnips, cabbage, green beans, peas, squash, tomatoes, cucumbers, butter beans. We planted the vegetables that we saw our parents plant all of our lives. I planned to preserve the vegetables as my mother had done. I decided to buy myself a pressure cooker, some glass jars for canning and preserve all of the vegetables that Guy and I needed for the winter months. Guy thought a chest-type freezer was best, so he bought one for us.

After moving into our house, Guy continued to work seven days a week. I would tell him sometimes that I wanted him to stay home from work at least one day a week. He would say that it was necessary, even more so than when we lived in Detroit, because no one will take care of your business for you, at least not anyone that he knew.

Guy had 8 brothers and I had 11 brothers. Barney was my favorite brother although he was eleven years older than I. He worked away from home, but came home on weekends when I was a little girl. When he came, he always brought Gertrude and me little gifts like hair bows, nail polish, candy and gum. We were always happy to see him coming. The gifts from him were why he was so special to me. I never remember Barney playing with us or even talking to us very much but he knew how to make a little girl happy. Even after he was married, he would bring us gifts when he visited.

Barney moved to West Virginia in the 1940's, where he got a job in a coal mine. His job was driving some kind of car that brought coal out of the mine. The brakes failed on the car, it crashed and he was killed. His body was sent home to be buried. Barney's wife Mattie and their two sons, Jesse and Franklin, were living in Alabama. At that time Guy and I only had one child. She was three at the time of Barney's death in 1956. Having a child of my own, I could know better how Papa felt. This was not his first son to be killed, but the fourth. For me, Barney's death was very upsetting, since he was so very special to me. But for Papa it had to be more devastating to him than I could really know. Barney was still a very young man, only about thirty-seven years of age.

After Barney was buried, my brothers who came to the funeral went back to West Virginia, Dayton, Ohio, and Atlanta, Georgia. My sister Lillie returned to her home in Columbus, Ohio. Gertrude and her family went home to Anniston, Alabama. Papa was very sad for a long time after Barney died but did not speak much about it at the time. Guy and I returned to our home in the next county which was not very far away from Papa's house.

Guy and I continued to work through the stress of the loss of a father and a brother. However, there was no time to dwell on the sadness because Guy and his brothers had many problems in their working situation at that time. The problems were not due to there being a shortage of trees to cut; but because they operating a business that black men did not commonly operate. In general, they were not trusted by the white people who would be purchasers of the lumber.

Many times Guy came home and told me what his day was like. Guy told me this story once, which was a common scenario: He said to me: 'we traveled today to look at a tract of timber that was for sale. When we approached the land owner, he asked us what white man we were buying it for. When he learned that we personally were seeking to purchase the timber, he increased the price so much that we could not afford to buy it. If we had bought it at his asking price, we could not have made any profit from it. So we had to look for a different tract timber'. Many times when they found timber that was not priced too high, it was so far away from home that when they went to cut it, they could not come home every night, but had to stay there until the weekend.

Once Guy told me how they had to sell lumber in Florida. He told me when they got to the lumber yard where lumber was purchased; the buyer asked who the lumber belonged to. Since most of the time they bought timber from white people, he would give the name of the person that they bought the timber from. Some places would refuse to buy the lumber if they knew that it belonged to a black-owned company. So they had to go to another lumber yard and look for someone that would buy it from them. They had similar problems the whole time that they operated that sawmill.

In 1963 they were able to buy a large track of timber from Tuskegee Institute, in Tuskegee, Alabama. That was about seventy five miles from our home in Malone, Alabama. Guy and his brothers began cutting timber around the first part of the year. Working so far away from home made it necessary for Guy to stay Monday through Friday in Tuskegee. Regina and Stacy were still small children. I was very unhappy when Guy worked in an area that required him to spend the night away from home. I was so afraid alone at night when he had to be away. After working there a few weeks, Guy rented an apartment in Tuskegee and moved Regina, Stacy, and myself to Tuskegee, to be with him.

Since there were so many family members depending on this one business, I began working to help out. My job was to cook for Guy and some of his workers there in Tuskegee. About three months after we moved there, Guy began building us another house in Tuskegee. Our children and I helped Guy build our house. Guy's brothers also helped us when they could take the time away from work. I helped Guy nail planks on the walls, and helped hang drywall. Regina and Stacy handed us nails as we needed them, and did whatever they could, when they were not in school. At the time only Regina attended school; since Stacy was only 5 years old. The work was tiring for me at times, but I did not mind it. While building our new house, we lived in an apartment complex named Mitchell Village; it was not a very nice place. Mitchell Village was actually barracks from the Air Force Base that was once in Tuskegee. They were then used as apartments for the general public. We were working to move away as soon as possible. We moved in our new house in the winter of 1963.

The first school that our daughter attended in Malone, before we moved to Tuskegee, was more primitive than the first school that I had attended twenty five years earlier. Woodville was the name of the school. Guy had attended that same school when he was a little boy just beginning school. It was a one room building, without running water, and an outside toilet. Children in grades one through six attended that school; and all six grades were taught by one teacher. That one teacher taught each of the grades every day through all the required subjects. One of the years that Regina attended there her teacher was a man Mr. Foster. The other two and half years her teacher was Mrs. Young, a very young lady just out of college.

A school bus came by our house that Regina could have ridden to school. It came really early because it also took the older children on to Wedowee to the high school. If she had ridden the bus every morning, Regina and the other children would just have to stand outside of the school and wait until the teacher got there. For that reason, I took her to school almost every morning and picked her up most afternoons.

We moved to Tuskegee when Regina was in the fourth grade. The school in Tuskegee was different than her old school in Malone, because there she had a teacher that taught only one grade. Regina had excellent teachers at her new school. The teachers said she was a very good student. Regina always enjoyed going to school, never wanted to miss a day of school. I didn't think that her new teacher ever knew about the one-room, one—teacher school that Regina attended just a few months before coming to Tuskegee.

Stacy had his sixth birthday after we moved to Tuskegee. Therefore, he never attended the one-room school. Once when he was about four, he decided that he wanted to go to school with his sister because when she went to school, he had no one to play with. I decided to let him go one day. I fixed him a lunch like Regina. He wanted books to take with him so I gave him some of the books that I had bought for him like 'The Three Little Pigs', 'Ba Ba Black Sheep' and 'Little Red Riding Hood'. Stacy was such a happy little boy going to school that day. I got permission for Regina's teacher to leave him at school. At twelve o'clock I thought I needed to see if he was enjoying being there and not being noisy or disrupting the class. When I arrived at the school, Stacy had gotten all of the school he wanted. He told me that he was ready to go home. He never asked again to go to school with his sister.

My son Stacy and his wife Belinda in 1984

The first September that we lived in Tuskegee, Stacy was six, and therefore, old enough to go to school. Some little boys that he played with everyday were starting to go to the same school that year. I was sure he would like it this time, but I was so wrong. Stacy hated school. Many days after getting him ready to catch the bus, he cried and said that he was too sick to go. On the occasions when I would let him stay at home, about thirty minutes after Regina had gone, he was ready to go outside and play. I knew then he was not really sick, so I would take him to school in my car. I hated the drive to school, because if he would start crying again, he looked so sad, then I wanted to cry. By the time he reached the third grade, he stopped crying and saying he was sick, but he never enjoyed school. He did his school work well, and never had to repeat a grade, but he when he graduated, was so pleased to be finished with school. He enjoyed working under a house, helping his Dad put in a Heating and Cooling Units, much more than he did going to school. He finished high school and two years of trade school. When he could go to work every day, that pleased him.

When Guy began working in Tuskegee, it was not the first time he had to cut timber so far away from home that he had to stay away overnight during the weekdays. The other times would be for only a few months; but not years as the job in Tuskegee would require. They once bought some timber in the mountains near Sylacauga, Alabama. I could not have gone with him then even if I had wanted to.

Guy and all the other workers lived together in an old house near the woods where the timber was located. They did their own cooking while working there. Once each week, my mother-in-law, Mrs. Marable, and the rest of us wives would cook a lot of food and carry it to them. It would take us about one and a half hours to drive to Sylacauga.

Our plans were to live in Tuskegee only for the two years that it required to cut that tract of timber, and then move back to Malone. All of the families were getting larger. Guy's younger brothers were by this time all married and raising children, as we were doing. They were all working hard, but the business was not enough for all of us.

My father-in-law, Mr. Marable was a smart, hard working man who knew how to build houses. His sons learned everything from him. I am sure he saw to them doing so. Mr. Marable was born in 1894. He only completed the third grade but had the abiltites of a contractor that had been trained to build houses. His sons learned to turn trees into lumber, and then lumber into houses, as he did. If a customer asked for a Spanish style house, a Colonial, or a Ranch style with two bedrooms, the Marable Brothers, as their company was named, would build it for them. They, like their father, had not been trained to do any of this work in school. Guy worked longer hours, once they started building house and continued to run the saw mill. Sometimes he complained that he needed eight days in the week, because there was so much to do.

When I cooked for the workers in Tuskegee, I was the only wife there. But a few months later, other wives and children moved to the area to join their husbands and fathers.

A few months after we moved to Tuskegee, my sister Gertrude began having health problems. She was at that time living in Anniston Alabama with her husband and three children. She became pregnant during the fall of 1963. Along with being pregnant, she was sick a lot. She carried her baby to term but she continued to be sick. That baby, Keith, was her second son and she now had a total of two boys and two girls. We lived over a hundred miles apart, but I knew she had to see her doctor often. Her doctor in Anniston sent her to the Mayo Clinic in Minnesota to have surgery for a problem with her kidneys when Keith was only five months old. She died during surgery. Her son Paul was ten years old, daughter Debra was twelve years old and her oldest daughter, Kaye was eighteen years old. Kaye was attending college at Tuskegee Institute, at the time of her mother's death. Kaye continued to attend college in Tuskegee making it possible for me to spend time with her often but the other three children I could not see very much since they lived so far away; but I visited them whenever I could.

Kaye graduated from college in 1967 and began working for Delta Airlines around 1970. If Gertrude was alive she would be enjoying three delightful grandchildren. Debra has a son named Brian; Paul has a son named Winston; and Keith's daughter is LaZavia. Kaye is more like a daughter to me than a niece. Her mother Gertrude married when she was really young, so when she became pregnant, she wanted to be home with our mother when her child was born. Kaye was cared for by Papa, Mama, Gertrude and I.

Gertrude's dying was such a tragedy. Not just because we loved her and her children needed her, but because she had not had a good or easy life for many years. Now at the age of thirty-six, she was dead. It seemed as if Papa's loosing his children would not end.

By this time, Guy, our children, and I had moved into our new house. All of his brother's families were by now in Tuskegee also. Only their mother, Mrs. Marable remained in Malone. Shortly after we moved into our house, Guy and his brothers began building their mother a house, and in 1964, she moved into her new house.

I ended my cooking job and then went to the Macon County Board of Education and applied for a job as a substitute teacher. I was given a job in a school very close to our home. Since I was only a substitute teacher, every day I had a different class. I worked at least three days each week that entire year. I did not have a college degree, so I was paid only ten dollars for everyday that I worked. That was a help for us then. Before school started again the next fall, a friend told me that if I wanted to work full time that I should apply at Tuskegee Institute as a house advisor in one of the freshmen dormitories. I liked the job and I needed to work. The main disadvantage was the fact that I was required to work the eleven p.m. to seven a.m. shift. That was not a good time for me because Regina was only eleven years old then and Stacy was seven. I wanted to be home early in the morning with them. Guy cooked breakfast everyday that I worked and did all he could to help the children get ready for school, but I wanted to be there to help with them. I worked that year, but not another one.

My next job came two weeks after school had ended that spring. The job was at the Veterans Canteen, at the Veteran Administration Hospital in Tuskegee. I worked on two other jobs. At two different times I worked at a sewing factory. At that job I made linings for all-weather coats. To make the amount of linings required, I had to sew as fast as possible all day. At the end of every day, my arms, shoulders and eyes were so tired. Many times I wished that I would have accepted Guy's offer to send me to college. Once I had to go to work after we move to Tuskegee, I had to work at whatever job I could find. Many of the jobs were really hard work and did not pay very much. I took them anyway because we needed the money.

All things considered, we managed financially and were able to care for our young family. We always owned our own home, which was nicely furnished; we owned a car and a pick-up; took the kids on vacations; and helped the rest of the family support Guy's mother.

To Live And To Die

When Guy and his brothers began building houses in the 1970's, they began to be commonly known as "Marable Brothers" than when they only were running the sawmill and selling lumber. There were seven brothers, including Guy, working together, running the sawmill, and building houses.

The foundations of the houses that they built, the framing and roofing were all done by all of the brothers together but the other features of the construction of the houses were done by individual ones of them. Guy and our son Stacy put all of the heating and cooling units in the houses. Guy's brother Vester and his son did the electrical work. The work that Guy and our son did was still a part of Marable Brothers Construction but was called, "Guy's Heating and Cooling".

Guy and Stacy did not only put all the heating and cooling units in the houses they built, but in houses that other contractors built also. For that reason they bought many Heating and Cooling Units from one company in Montgomery, Alabama. That company gave each of their buyers and the buyer's wife an all expense paid trip some place in September of each year. To receive the trip, they were required to buy a particular dollar amount of heating and cooling units to qualify for the trip. That kind of traveling was very new to Guy and me. Our traveling in the past was trips to Ohio and Michigan to visit relatives or the few hours that we had spent in Canada. We would always get the encyclopedias that we had for our children and read about the country that we were going to before going there.

During all of the great trips to far-away places I would think of Mama and Papa and how much they would have enjoyed seeing these places and knowing that these places did not just exist in books, but were real.

One trip that we received was to Mexico City and Acapulco Mexico. Soon after we arrived in Mexico City, we observed that many people still lived in poverty. People lived there in shacks made of cardboard boxes; others were built from cement blocks with flat roofs made of sheet metal or straw. Some of the houses that we saw only had one room and a hard-packed dirt floor. The kitchen of some of the houses was simply a lean-to built of poles and cornstalks placed against an outside wall.

Our tour guide explained many facts about the large city and the country. When we stopped at different shops, most any item you might think of for decorating or jewelry you could see it there made from silver. While we were in Mexico City our tour took us to many different places, religious temples and while there we would see people worshiping their images and idols. Inside of one of the religious buildings, we saw people bowing to and praying to the Virgin of Guadalupe, the patron saint of Mexico. We were told that nearly all of Mexico's people belong to the Roman Catholic Church. The people followed their ancient customs and lived much as their ancestors did before the white man arrived.

We were taken to see the pyramids in Mexico City also. To get to one there, we went out of the city to what looked like a desert. It was called the Pyramid of the Sun and it covered more than ten acres and was said to be 20 feet high.

Bullfighting is the most popular spectator sport in Mexico. Mexico City has the largest bullfighting arena in the world which seats about 50,000 people although we did not get to see that one.

One of the more interesting parts of our trip was our bus ride from Mexico City to Acapulco. Every village town had a market place. There men, women and children had their clothes, food, lace, pictures, toys, baskets and other items to sell or trade. Mexican villagers followed the older way of life more than the city people. The bus went around and up the mountains. When getting near the top of one, that was the last one before going down into Acapulco, we were by then riding in clouds. When looking out of the windows of the bus, Guy and I as well as the others saw some clouds below us. I had ridden above the clouds before in a plane but to see them while still on the ground in this way was exciting to see.

We traveled through the desert before getting to the mountains, there were cactuses of all sized and some were really tall and beautiful. Before getting to Acapulco, we stopped at a town by the name of Taxco, Mexico. It was not a large town but after just leaving Mexico City with a population of many million people, it was more likely larger than it seemed to be. There were so many gift shops in that town, with unusual gifts displayed. While there, Guy bought me a necklace, bracelet and earrings to match that were made from silver and abalone and are still very pretty more than twenty years later. While there we saw furniture in one of the shops made from Onyx marble, it was like nothing I had ever seen before.

After we arrived in Acapulco we were carried to a mountain that was near the ocean and while there we watched cliff divers jumping into water far below them. They were exciting to watch. On that same day we watched a bull fight, the matador treated the bull so bad that Guy and I could not watch it to the end. We went outside and waited for the others that were on our tour bus.

We also had a five hour cruise in the Pacific Ocean that I enjoyed so much. Guy was so sure that he would get sea sickness that he did not allow himself to enjoy the cruise. He did not get sick at all. After spending four days in Mexico City and three in Acapulco we were both ready to go home.

Another trip that they gave us was to San Juan, Puerto Rico which was a beautiful, fertile island about a thousand miles southeast of Florida. It forms part of the boundary between the Atlantic Ocean and the Caribbean Sea. Puerto Ricans are U.S. citizens and can move to the mainland without immigration restrictions. I can only remember going shopping those first days to buy souvenirs. Afterward we went on our tour bus to a resort hotel about twenty or thirty miles out of San Juan. There we stayed at a beautiful hotel on the beach. Walking on the beach and sitting around the pool there was so relaxing. Guy was able to get the much needed rest that he couldn't get back home. At night we could hear the waves hitting the shore and the sounds were so soothing. I remember the food at the hotel was delicious. In the hotel lobby was a Coral Reef that was at least five feet tall. Guy made pictures of it since I had been collecting small ones to take home.

Another time we were given a trip to Las Vegas, Nevada. We stayed at the MGM Grand Hotel and saw a live show every night. Shopping in the Hotel there was like shopping at a fabulous mall in Atlanta. While there in Las Vegas, a tour was arranged for us to visit Hoover Dam, one of the highest dams in the world. It stands in the Black Canyon of the Colorado River. It controls the floods of the Colorado River and supplies domestic irrigation water and electric power for a large area of the Pacific Southwest.

By the 1970's, the Marable Brothers were no longer cutting any timber. In 1973 they heard about timber being so plentiful in Liberia Africa. Liberia is the oldest Negro republic in Africa and the second oldest in the world. Liberia became a free nation more than 110 years before any other county in tropical Africa. Since one of the chief products at that time was forest products, the Marable Brothers were interested in that country. They heard that timber there was being sold for much less than timber was sold for here in the United States. They decided if they could go there, buy some of it and then buy themselves another sawmill because by this time they no longer had one. They would go there and work for a while sawmilling again.

Soon after receiving this news, Guy plus two of his brothers and their attorney went there to get a look at the timber. I was so excited about the possibility that maybe if they did work for a while that Guy would let Stacy and me come there later, once they had worked for a while.

Regina by this time was married and living in Atlanta, Georgia. I decided if he would go there and let Stacy and I come and stay with him, we could then send for Gina to come and visit us in Africa for a while.

They stayed only one week in Liberia, when he returned home, Guy had so much to tell about Liberia. He brought me two beautiful dresses from there, and brought gifts also for Regina and Stacy. We would have gatherings after he came home because different ones in the family wanted to hear Guy talk about Africa. After Guy and I went to bed at night, he continued to tell me things about his trip.

They went to different villages while there and saw how primitive their lifestyle was. They saw women washing their clothes in the rivers. Some of the homes of the people had dirt floors. Something that was so amazing to him was that the homes were so clean. The weather there was warm most of the time, so different fruits and vegetables grew year round.

After getting back home, they had to wait to hear about what was going to be decided about the work. Plans were never worked out in a way that would benefit them if they returned to Africa to cut timber.

The temperatures in Liberia average about 80 degrees year round. Papa was still alive when Guy went to Africa and when he told him about the warm weather, Papa asked if people farm year round there. Guy told him that the people worked at other jobs as well as farming. Some were fisherman and others tapped trees for rubber and others raised cattle. Papa had never before heard that rubber came from trees. He believed what Guy told him but was so amazed. Guy asked Papa did he remember how he used to get tar from pine trees and that it was similar to the way rubber is taken from trees.

After my niece Kaye began working for Delta Airlines, we traveled to more interesting places with her. She once took me and Guy to Hawaii on a trip that I will never forget. We traveled on a Delta jet from Atlanta to Los Angeles. We had to change airlines there because in the 1970's Delta did not fly to Hawaii.

We toured the island of Oahu on our first day there. Our tour guide explained to us a little of the history of the state. One fact being that Honolulu is the state capital and the largest city is Oahu. Before preparing to go to Hawaii, all I remembered about the state was that it was made up of islands in the Pacific Ocean and Pearl Harbor was there.

The tour guide also told us that Hawaii was made up of more than 100 islands and those geographers divided the islands into three groups: eight main islands in the southwest, islets of rock in the middle and coral and sand islands in the northwest. And that all islands were formed by volcanoes built up from the ocean floor.

I had read a little about Hawaii in the encyclopedia and that information was a help to me in understanding the things that the tour guide told us. The climate of Hawaii is pleasantly mild all year long. While in Hawaii, we went to a farm where pineapples grew and to the Dole Pineapple factory where we were served fresh pineapples and pineapple juice.

We traveled by plane from Honolulu to the large island Hawaii to visit the volcanoes national park. It was a little scary to watch nature at work of earth building. The Polynesians were the first people to live in Hawaii. They sailed there from other Pacific islands along with other Polynesian people who moved to the island from Tahiti about 1200 A.D. We visited the Polynesian Cultural Center near Laie on Oahu that included six Polynesian villages inhabited by people from Fiji and Tonga Island, Hawaii, New Zealand, Samoa and Tahiti. We were entertained by them with their songs and dances. The tour of that center lasted for about eight hours and it was not the least bit boring.

In 1979, Guy made it possible for me to visit a place often referred to as the Holy Land which is in Israel. The trip began in Atlanta and I was to meet at the JFK Airport in New York the group that I spent the next nine days with. Including me it was 102 of us in the group. We traveled non-stop from New York to Amsterdam Holland. That took seven hours of flying time. We spent four hours in Amsterdam before traveling on to Israel's largest city and major industrial center, Tel Aviv-Yafa.

We were met by our tour guide that escorted us to our bus. We were taken to a hotel in New Jerusalem and assigned rooms there because we were to stay there for four nights and three days. We visited old Jerusalem, Bethlehem and on to the Dead Sea, the lowest place on the earth.

Our tour guide was Jewish, but he told us that he had lived in California for about five years and that he had read the Watchtower magazine on a regular basis. He told us if he knew a little about Jehovah's Witnesses then he could know what places and things about Israel that would interest us the most.

99

While walking along the street with our guide, he mentioned how it was thought by some persons there that Jesus Christ might have walked on the same street nearly 2,000 years before.

Our bus stopped when we got to the Salt Sea, we were allowed to get out of the bus, walk down to the sea. Some in the group took their shoes off and walked in the shallow water at the edges of the sea. Some people there think that salt sea formed from Gomorrah. The guide reminded us that it is not a proven fact.

While still in Jerusalem we went to the Jews Ancient Holy Wailing Wall. The people there, some were praying near the wall and some were putting folded pieces of paper in cracks in the walls. We were told that prayers were written on the papers they were leaving there.

The religion of the Jews there ranged from those who were Orthodox, to those with no religious beliefs. About 80 percent of the country's Arabs are Moslems and the rest are Christians. The people in Israel celebrate holy days according to four calendars. The Jews follow the Hebrew calendar and the Moslems observe the Islamic calendar. Christian holy days are celebrated according to either the Gregorian of the Julian calendar.

When we were there the population of the whole country was only a little over three million. In that same year Israel had only four cities with a population over one hundred thousand. Our last three nights there in Israel, we stayed in a hotel in Haifa. While there our touring took us to the Sea of Galilee. We went across the sea on a boat that was arranged for us. We were reminded of the Bible account that is recorded in Matthew 14:24-26. According to the New World Translation of the Holy Scriptures: verse 24 By now the boat was many hundreds of yards away from land, being hard put to it by the waves, because the wind was against them. 25: But in the fourth watch period of the night he came to them, walking over the sea. 26 When they caught sight of him walking on the sea;

the disciples were troubled, saying: "it is an apparition! And they cried out in their fear. Before going to Israel, I had never had any doubts about anything written in the Scriptures about Jesus was not inspired and true. But to be there at those particular places made these accounts more real to me.

From the Sea of Galilee we traveled next to Nazareth. Our guide knew our reason for thinking of that city as being the place where Jesus grew up. He had read the account of Joseph being told in a dream to take Mary his wife and Jesus away from Bethlehem, because Herod the king was searching for Jesus to kill him, because he had heard that this child that had been born was to become a king.

Our guide was stating what the Bible says about this in Matthew 2:1-23.

> 1 After Jesus had been born in Beth'le·hem of Ju·de'a in the days of Herod the king, look! Astrologers from eastern parts came to Jerusalem, 2 saying: "Where is the one born king of the Jews? For we saw his star [when we were] in the east, and we have come to do him obeisance." 3 At hearing this King Herod was agitated, and all Jerusalem along with him; 4 and on gathering together all the chief priests and scribes of the people he began to inquire of them where the Christ was to be born. 5 They said to him: "In Beth'le·hem of Ju·de'a; for this is how it has been written through the prophet, 6 'And you, O Beth'le·hem of the land of Judah, are by no means the most insignificant [city] among the governors of Judah; for out of you will come forth a governing one, who will shepherd my people, Israel.'"
> 7 Then Herod secretly summoned the astrologers and carefully ascertained from them the time of the star's appearing; 8 and, when sending them to Beth'le·hem, he said: "Go make a careful search for the young child, and

when YOU have found it report back to me, that I too may go and do it obeisance." **9** When they had heard the king, they went their way; and, look! the star they had seen [when they were] in the east went ahead of them, until it came to a stop above where the young child was. **10** On seeing the star they rejoiced very much indeed. **11** And when they went into the house they saw the young child with Mary its mother, and, falling down, they did obeisance to it. They also opened their treasures and presented it with gifts, gold and frankincense and myrrh. **12** However, because they were given divine warning in a dream not to return to Herod, they withdrew to their country by another way.

13 After they had withdrawn, look! Jehovah's angel appeared in a dream to Joseph, saying: "Get up, take the young child and its mother and flee into Egypt, and stay there until I give you word; for Herod is about to search for the young child to destroy it." **14** So he got up and took along the young child and its mother by night and withdrew into Egypt, **15** and he stayed there until the decease of Herod, for that to be fulfilled which was spoken by Jehovah through his prophet, saying: "Out of Egypt I called my son."

16 Then Herod, seeing he had been outwitted by the astrologers, fell into a great rage, and he sent out and had all the boys in Beth'le·hem and in all its districts done away with, from two years of age and under, according to the time that he had carefully ascertained from the astrologers. **17** Then that was fulfilled which was spoken through Jeremiah the prophet, saying: **18** "A voice was heard in Ra'mah, weeping and much wailing; it was Rachel weeping for her children, and she was unwilling to take comfort, because they are no more."

19 When Herod had deceased, look! Jehovah's angel appeared in a dream to Joseph in Egypt **20** and said: "Get up, take the young child and its mother and be on your way into the land of Israel, for those who were seeking the soul of the young child are dead." **21** So he got up and took the young child and its mother and entered into the land of Israel. **22** But hearing that Ar·che·la′us ruled as king of Ju·de′a instead of his father Herod, he became afraid to depart for there. Moreover, being given divine warning in a dream, he withdrew into the territory of Gal′i·lee, **23** and came and dwelt in a city named Naz′a·reth, that there might be fulfilled what was spoken through the prophets: "He will be called a Naz·a·rene′."

Our tour also took us to the Jordan River. The tour guide mentioned another account in the Bile that he thought might interest us. The account is recorded in Joshua 3:1-17. That tells of the miracle they experienced when crossing the river. How the waters dammed up so the Israelites could get into the land that God had promised to give to them. This is the account as it is recorded in Chapter 3 verses 1-17:

> **1** Then Joshua got up early in the morning, and he and all the sons of Israel proceeded to pull away from Shit′tim and to come as far as the Jordan; and they went spending the night there before they would cross.
> **2** So it came about at the end of the three days that the officers proceeded to pass through the midst of the camp **3** and to command the people, saying: "As soon as YOU see the ark of the covenant of Jehovah YOUR God, and the priests, the Levites, carrying it, then YOU yourselves will pull away from YOUR place, and YOU must follow it, **4** —only let their prove to be a distance between YOU and it of about two thousand cubits by measure; do not get near to it—in order that YOU may know the way by which YOU should go, for YOU have not passed over on that way before."

5 Joshua now said to the people: "Sanctify yourselves, for tomorrow Jehovah will do wonderful things in YOUR midst."

6 Then Joshua said to the priests: "Take up the ark of the covenant and pass before the people." So they took up the ark of the covenant and went before the people.

7 And Jehovah proceeded to say to Joshua: "This day I shall start to make you great in the eyes of all Israel, that they may know that just as I proved to be with Moses I shall prove to be with you. **8** And you—you should command the priests carrying the ark of the covenant, saying, 'As soon as YOU have come as far as the edge of the waters of the Jordan, YOU should stand still in the Jordan.'"

9 And Joshua went on to say to the sons of Israel: "Approach here and listen to the words of Jehovah YOUR God." **10** After that Joshua said: "By this YOU will know that a living God is in YOUR midst, and that he will without fail drive away from before YOU the Ca′naan·ites and the Hit′tites and the Hi′vites and the Per′iz·zites and the Gir′ga·shites and the Am′or·ites and the Jeb′u·sites. **11** Look! The ark of the covenant of the Lord of the whole earth is passing before YOU into the Jordan. **12** And now take for yourselves twelve men from the tribes of Israel, one man for each tribe. **13** And it must occur that at the instant that the soles of the feet of the priests carrying the ark of Jehovah, the Lord of the whole earth, rest in the waters of the Jordan, the waters of the Jordan will be cut off, the waters descending from above, and they will stand still as one dam."

14 And it came about that when the people pulled away from their tents just before passing over the Jordan, with the priests carrying the ark of the covenant before the people, **15** and at the instant that the carriers of the Ark came as far as the Jordan and the feet of the priests carrying the Ark were dipped in the edge of the waters (now the Jordan overflows all its banks all the days of harvest), **16** then the waters descending from above began to stand still. They rose up as one dam very far away at Adam, the city at the side of Zar´e·than, while those descending toward the sea of the Ar´a·bah, the Salt Sea, were exhausted. They were cut off, and the people passed over in front of Jer´i·cho. **17** Meanwhile the priests carrying the ark of Jehovah's covenant kept standing immovable on dry ground in the middle of the Jordan as all Israel were passing over on dry ground, until the whole nation had completed passing over the Jordan.

The day then came that we were to leave Israel after seven memorable days that I would never forget. We went back to Tel-Aviv to get our flight that was to take us first back to Amsterdam, then on the New York and for me on to Atlanta. While waiting in the airport in Tel-Aviv to board our plane, we were all asked calmly to leave the waiting area, and to go out of the airport. We obeyed the orders and once outside we were told that someone had called and said a bomb was in the airport. That was really upsetting to us. About thirty minutes later after a careful search was made it was found not to be true.

We boarded our plane as soon as we went back inside. Our plane left as soon as we were all accounted for. Fourteen hours later, I was back in Atlanta and so anxious to get back home. I have many souvenirs that I brought back from Israel that are still reminders to me of that trip.

Stacy began working with his father when he was really young. Guy grew up on a farm as I did and as I did began helping in the fields when he was a little boy. Guy was still cutting lumber at the sawmill and Stacy went to the mill after school every afternoon and on Saturdays to work.

During the summer months when school was out he worked every day. I think that even before Stacy finished high school he enjoyed working with his father. There were times that he most likely wanted to be playing with boys his age that did not hit a lick at a snake the whole summer. Since their fathers were not self employed as Stacy's father was, they had nothing for them to do every day. Stacy never complained about the work he always obeyed his father, he got up early every morning went to work just as Guy did.

In Stacy's last year of high school, he went to school only half of the day, and the other half he went to trade school. Alabama Technical Trade School was in Opelika, Alabama. After finishing high school, he then needed only to attend that trade school for one more year. At the school he was studying installation of heating and cooling units. He also was learning to repair refrigerators. He had already some on the job training, working with his father.

Guy was determined that he have a certificate in that work. He wanted him to be able to get jobs on his own and have the means or the certificate to prove to whoever he needed to that he could do the work.

Stacy is now married and lives about 100 miles away. He and his wife Belinda are parents to four beautiful children; three sons and one daughter. My granddaughter is the oldest of the four, Ellen Marie is her name and the sons are Stacy Jr., Jonathan and Troy Oliver. They are four delightful and loving children. Once, I vacationed at Sandestin Beach, Florida with Stacy and his family. When I spend time with them, I almost feel young again. It is such a joy to spend a night with Stacy and his family. Troy, who was three years old at the time, would sometimes sleep with me. He liked for me to make up stories about rabbits, dogs, monkeys and other animals, and I would always include him in the story.

My children were now in their fifties. Their personalities are so different. Seeing them together, anyone could see right away that they are sister and brother. Our daughter is five feet tall and weighs about 100 pounds. Our son is five feet and eleven inches tall and weighs about 200 pounds.

When beginning to write some of my memories down on paper, they were to be of my parents primarily and growing up with them, being trained and molded by them and remembering how I felt about what they were like as parents. Children today and their relationships with their parents are so different to my relationship was with mine. I have so many times told Regina and Stacy that I wished my parents had lived and our houses were close enough together for the two of them to have spent time each day with them. I wanted to raise my own children, but for them also to have training from my Papa and Mama. That would have been good for my children.

When Guy and I were raising our children, our lifestyle was so different to our parents. We worked away from home and we were away from them so much. We did not have that togetherness. I feel now my children missed out on a lot in many ways. I didn't think at that time that we were neglecting them in any way. We worked hard to provide for them and ourselves. We gave them all the love that we knew how. Stacy continues to operate the business that he and his father created for themselves as building contractors.

In July 1989, Guy had started a job in Opelika, Alabama. Remodeling someone's home and completed much of the job. He went to work that day as usual and was on the job all day. When he came home that afternoon he told me that he had indigestion and asked me to fix an Alka Seltzer to take before eating dinner. I fixed it and he took it. About fifteen minutes later he told me the pain in his chest was not getting any better. I asked him to let me take him to the emergency room and see a doctor. He didn't think he needed a doctor and asked if I had anything else for indigestion. I gave him two Maalox tables but by then he was having difficulty breathing and I called 911 for help and they came about fifteen minutes later but by then Guy had stopped breathing.

The paramedics tried over and over to revive him and I was thinking that he would start breathing again any second but he never did. I could not believe that Guy had died. It was not real to me then, it was almost as if I was watching something tragic on television. The ambulance came to take him away from home. Then only was it real to me. They were not taking him to a doctor, he had died. He had a massive heart attack. I did not know what to do. It was like a part of me was dead and I became so weak that my head started to ache and it did not stop for days afterward.

Losing my parents was devastating to me but losing my husband was almost unbearable. For a long time I could not understand why that was true. I thought the love was the same. I loved my parents as much as I could and I thought it was the same with my husband. But I started to remember when you get married to someone you become one flesh with that one. Being one flesh with Guy meant we were supposed to be at unity and in agreement. He was to love me as he did himself and I was to have deep respect for him. He was my head. I lost my headship, someone to love me, to provide for me and to protect me.

I now had no one to be in subjection to and no one to have deep respect for. I did not lose that with my parents or anyone else. When my parents died I still had a family but I did not when Guy died. My children come to see me and I go to their home occasionally and then return home after a day or two. Not only do I feel sad for myself but I feel sad and still feel sad for Guy. He has no memory now, no feelings, and no knowledge because in death all thought perish. Psalms 146:4 says: "His spirit goes out, he goes back to his ground, in that day his thoughts do perish'"

When Guy died I am sure that is not what he wanted to happen to him. He died in the way he had for many years said that he hoped he would die, because he did not want to be sick for a long time as some people are and for me to have to care for him. He often said that he didn't want to be a burden to anyone at anytime. I think about it sometimes since I am now almost seventy years old. When I go to the nursing homes and see so many helpless sick people, some of them do not even know where they are or who they are. I feel so sad for them. I just want to go away someplace and just cry for a whole day or until all of these sorrows go away.

I continued to live in Tuskegee nearly three years after Guy died before I moved back to my hometown of Roanoke Alabama. Although Roanoke was my hometown, I never lived in the city limits of Roanoke before.

My parent's farm was about five miles from Roanoke, but this was the town we always came to. When Guy was alive, we had decided that one day we would move back and build a house in what used to be the hog pasture on Papa and Mama's farm. His parent's farm was not far away. At that time Guy was raising cows and he said he would take them once we moved to his parents place in Randolph County.

When I began planning to move to Roanoke my circumstances had changed and the reason for wanting to move had changed. All of the decisions to be made had to be mine and mine alone. Finding a place to build the house that was to be my new home was my responsibility. My daughter and son came with me a time or two to assist me in deciding where to build the house. Finding the right location, selecting the house plan was so enjoyable, it was fun and exciting to me. I was making plans to move away from Tuskegee and I was almost in a hurry to get away from there. There were so many memories there that I was having difficulties dealing with it. Moving away did not eliminate them, but I thought some distance away might help.

I drove up to this place so many times while the house was under construction. After the foundation was laid, I told Stacy that was such a pretty foundation. He laughed and said that he had never seen a pretty foundation for a house. Then the frame was completed and I knew that it was going to be a house. The roof was put on and I could then see more of the design of the house. Each time that I went there something new had been added. I drove from Tuskegee at least once every week. My son was building the house as he had helped his father in the past build houses for us. This time he was doing all of the work without Guy. I often wondered what he would think of what we were doing.

Soon after the outside walls were completed, Stacy asked me to go to different stores in Montgomery and select appliances, bathroom fixtures, light fixtures and other things that he knew that I wanted to select to be put inside the house. That was a pleasure to do. Then it came the time to select paint colors and kitchen cabinets.

I was making plans and working with a reality company in Tuskegee that was helping me to sell my home there. All of that kept me so busy and that was good for me. After about five months the house was completed. I had packed and labeled so many boxes, preparing to leave my home in Tuskegee and move to Roanoke.

I had never moved into a house all by myself before and did not realize what a responsibility that it would be. I soon realized that was the biggest job I had ever attempted to do. The day that I moved, the movers brought everything that I owned and put it in this house in exactly the place that I asked them to and then left me. That was what they were supposed to do; I was then all alone with no one to help me do anything.

I came as close as I ever did in my whole life to having a panic attack. I thought about my house in Tuskegee and who would take care of it until the sale was completed. The insurance company said they could only continue to cover it unoccupied for one month.

I survived those months but I still get chills sometimes when I thought about them.

I would sometimes go up to the house that Guy first built for us sometimes because it was only about fifteen miles from my new home in Roanoke. I had not seen the inside of the house since we moved away in 1963 and no one is ever there at the house when I go to it. Guy and I sold the house to Mr. David Hill in 1964 and he still owns it but does not live there now. I never go there alone because the county has changed the road up near the house. The road no longer goes by the house. Between the new road and the house, trees have grown up now you can no longer see it until you drive down a dirt road and now the house sits back in the woods.

The house is still pretty to me. No one would describe it that way but me. Maybe I see it as pretty because of the memories I have of living there. Both Regina and Stacy were born when we lived there. We began learning to be parents when we lived in that house. Once I walked around to the back yard, many memories started to come back to me. When we lived there we had a well that we got water from and it is no longer there, but I remember where in the yard that it stood. Out a little distance from the well, Guy built a barn in back of the barn in front of the cow pasture. After Guy built the barn and pasture, he bought three beautiful young Holstein cows; each of which were about to give birth to their first calf.

When they gave birth to their babies, they were so pretty. We only let them take milk from the cows for a few months, then bought a milk substitute from them and bottle feed the calves. That was a new experience for me. Our plans were to sell milk to the Carnation Company as Mrs. Marable, Guy's mother, was doing. The milk that we did not need for our own use, we put it in large cans that were provided for us by that company.

If the weather was hot, the milk cans after the milk had been put in them, had to be put in a tub of cold water, then put out beside the road. Early in the morning the man driving the Carnation Company's truck picked it up and put it on the truck and took it away. Once each month we received pay for the milk.

In a separate fence, Guy fixed a place to keep pigs that grew to be hogs by the winter time. They are raised to be slaughtered for meat. The hams, sausages and bacon were so good to us. Getting the hams and bacon cured that Guy did in salt making the sausages and doing the other work that was involved was no small task.

We raised chickens when we lived in that house. In the spring time, Guy planted corn and hay to have feed for the cows so he did not have to buy so much feed from the store for the animals and chickens along with that he went to the woods every day to cut trees down to make into lumber.

If I could buy that house back from Mr. Hill, I would try and decorate each room as I did when we moved into it more than forty years ago. Guy bought me a beautiful white, wood home comfort stove to use to cook on in the winter months. It kept the kitchen warm and we had no other heat in the kitchen. When summer came, Guy bought me an electric stove to use because the wood stove made the kitchen too hot in the summer. The wood stove and the electric stove stood side by side in our kitchen.

A fire place was in the living room, that heated the room and wood heaters were used to heat the other rooms. For that house I would want that same arrangement. If I got the opportunity to do that at the end of the project, I would probably be lonely as before because of missing my family no one would care about it but me, and no one would see it hardly ever, except me. For me it would all be worth it to do.

After growing up in a large family, a family with a father, mother, brothers and sisters, when there were never any fighting or abuse; then to have my own family, a husband and two loving children, then to be left alone, does not get any easier as the years pass. This is how I sometimes described what it likes to live alone after Guy died and left me.

> "What living alone is like
> Sometimes I feel like I'm in prison
> As one might think living there would be
> Or on some lonely desert island where someone had
> left me
> While in this confinement, each day seems like two
> This feeling is not true for all people who are
> Left alone like me
> For them, life goes on almost as it used to be
> Some days I feel lonely, as if I am the only person alive
> Even when I'm in the company with others, I feel
> invisible at times.
> Or if someone sees me, it's like I am a stranger, or in
> the way.
> So living alone for me it is far from being in
> A desirable way"

Our creator said it is not good for a person to be alone. Sometimes I feel that I am watching this person, myself, but I no longer know who she is. I was a daughter, a sister, a wife, a mother and now a widow; but the widow is not easy to identify. I work at my purpose for being alive, and I have goals that I try never to neglect. I enjoy living and have the desire to live forever, but I still miss having a family.

At the present time, I am restoring a quilt that Mama made more than fifty years ago. The quilt pattern is that of a sunflower, but Mama did not use the colors of that flower only, she used a variety of colors that made it so pretty. When she completed the flower design, using black embroidering thread she attached the sunflower to a white square block of material. The embroidery stitch that she used, she called it a brier stitch.

That thread is now pulled out in places. Mama taught me to do all the different hand crafting that she did except for the dress making. This embroidering is very time consuming. Once a block is completed it is very pretty. When I finish this work I plan to use this quilt as a wall hanging.

Memories of a brother of mine by the name of Booker stirred in my thinking today. But I'm sorry to say that there are not very many of them. One reason for that is we never lived in the same state after I reached the age of remembering things. Booker went to West Virginia, as many of my brothers did. He got a job in one of the coal mines as the others did. Sometimes I heard Mama and Papa say after coming home from a visit there. Booker worked in one there for a long time, then moved to the state of New York. His wife and children also went there to live. After moving there, I don't ever remember him coming home again to visit. That is another reason for having such few memories of him. He came home when our mother died in 1950, but when Papa died twenty four years later, for some reason he did not come to his funeral.

During the many years that Papa was in poor health he never came to visit him even once. Since I am a parent now, I can imagine how much that must have hurt him. Booked died in New York in 1987 at almost seventy years old. I am in fairly good health as of right now, but I still want and need to see my children and to know that they are well.

Lepolion was the one to see our brother Donnie be killed. Many times as I grew older I wanted to ask him what he was thinking as he ran behind the mule trying to catch him what was he thinking and saying to himself. Lepolion never mentioned it in my presence so I did not ask him questions that might upset him.

Lepolion went into the Army in 1942 and got married in 1944. He and his wife Helen raised seven children. He lived in Atlanta for fifty years and even before getting married. He was wounded and spent about one year in the hospital in Atlanta. In 1992, he decided that he wanted to move back to our hometown of Roanoke just as I had. He moved about six month before I moved back to Roanoke. Lepolion's health was not good when he moved to Roanoke. High blood pressure was a problem for him, he had three light strokes and was having a blood circulation problem in his legs. One of his legs was amputated as a result of the poor circulation problem. His health problems just would not end. His doctor made plans to amputate the other leg but before they could do so, he had a heart attack and died in January of 1995.

When one of my siblings dies, I think about my parents even more than usual. They married over 100 years ago, became parents to eleven sons and three daughters. As of 2011, only 2 of those children are alive; myself and one brother.

It's nearing the end of November and our weather is getting cold. Most days I enjoy a fire in the fireplace. The only fireplace that I have is in the living room. When I started using it, I arranged the furniture different in that room. Now that fireplace becomes the focal point in that room. To keep the fire going, I am, it seems, always going into the garage for wood.

I had my bedroom furniture arranged differently about a month ago. When I change the furniture around in any room, I always remember when Guy and I moved into our first house, I could rearrange the furniture all by myself, because the floors were all wood and moving the bed, dresser, or chest from one place to another was easy. When I moved our bed around or put it near another wall, what it did to Guy was always so funny to me. When he needed to get up at night to go to the bathroom, he would not be able to find it. Since he was half asleep, he would try to open the window or go into the closet, a he searched for the bathroom. He was lost in the room for a few seconds. I would always ask him to turn the light on and he would say that if I would stop moving our bed he could find what he needed to find in the dark.

Our next house had carpet on the bedroom floors, and because of that, I could not move the furniture without someone's help. When I asked Guy to help me he would talk me out of doing it most of the time. He never minded helping me move any other furniture around to different places but would say that he had gotten used to the bed right where it was and he would get lost at night in the house if I moved the bed.

I would then rearrange the pictures on the walls, change the curtains on the windows and paint the walls a different color. Guy soon learned that for me to move things around gave me a lift. To me it was almost like I had bought something new for the house. Many times when Guy was alive, he said that I would marry again and not continue alone when he died. He would say that I was an attractive lady and if I did not think so I would not have married you. He would say that I took good care of myself, kept a clean house and that I would be married in a few months. Now, wouldn't he be surprised that many years have passed and I am still Grace Marable. I think that this poem applies to me:

Last chance for love
My last chance for love has ended, the way I would
want it to be
I could only be a wife and happy if I'm treated special
by a man that loves me
To all people it's not necessary to have true love and
romance in life
It's thought by some, that once you have grown older
you
Should be happy and content with a companion, and
to someone be a wife
For me I could never let that happen, I would rather be
alone and blue
I could never pretend to be happy, without someone
special and true

I once thought time would make a difference, but it
has not
Proved to be true
Time has only made me older not closer to some
special and true

Once I wanted a canopy over our bed, but did not want to buy a canopy bed. I showed Guy one in a catalog like I wanted and asked him to build one for me. He built just what I needed using four pieces of lumber. He nailed each piece to the ceiling in our room directly over each side of the bed and then one piece of lumber over the headboard, the last piece was put over the foot of the bed. Each measured just the same as the width and length of the bed. The lumber that he used was two inches thick and four inches wide.

After they were nailed up and painted, Guy fastened curtain rods and brackets to the pieces of lumber. That was all that I needed him to do for me as I could complete the sewing of the curtains to create my canopy. Guy thought that in a year or two that I would ask him to take it down. I changed the colors sometimes with different material or sheets but when I sold that house, that canopy frame was still there.

Guy could do most anything that he put his mind to and wanted to do. Once we needed a set of twin beds. I showed him a set in a decorator magazine and he built them exactly like the one in the book. He once built us a couch for the living room. He built outdoor furniture for other people as well as for us. Many times one of his brothers would tell him that what he was about to do cannot be done but he would do it and do it very well.
The poem written by Edgar A. Guest titled "It couldn't be done" very well described my husband to me.

Someone said it couldn't be done, but he with a
chuckle replied
That may be it couldn't but he would be one who
wouldn't say
So until he tried
So he buckled to it, with a trace of a grin on his face,
if he
Worried he hid it.
He started to sing as he tackled the ting that
Couldn't be done and he did it.
Somebody scoffed, o' you'll never do that at least no
one had
Done it, but he took off his coat and he took off his
hat, and the first
Thing we knew he had begun it.
With the lift of his chin and a bit of a grin, without
any
Doubting or quitting. He started to sing as he tackled
the thing that
Couldn't be done and he did it.
There are thousands to tell you it cannot be done there
are
Thousands to prophesy failure, there are thousands to
point out to
You one by one the dangers that wait to assail you
But just buckle in with a grin, just take off your coat
and go to it. Just start to sing as you tackle the thing
that cannot be done
And you'll do it.

I always enjoyed reading poems. Many times I would read one to
Guy. One in particular I would read to him, the title of that one was
"Will you love me when I am old".

I will ask you my darling, a question soft and low, that
give
Me many heartache as the moments come and o.
Your love I know is truthful, but the truest love grows
cold; it
Is this that I would ask you: Will you love me when I
am old?
Life mom will soon be waning, and its evening bells be
tolled.
But my heart shall know no sadness, if you love me
when I'm old.
Down the stream of life together, we are sailing side by
side,
Hoping some bright day to anchor safe beyond the
surging tide,
Today our sky is cloudless, but the night may clouds
unfold;
But, through storms may gather round us, will you love
me when I'm old?
When my hair shall shade the snowdrift and my eyes
shall
Dimmer grow?
I would lean upon some loved one, through the valley
as I go.
I would claim of your promise, worth to me a world of
gold;
It is only this, my darling, that you'll love me when I'm
old.

After reading it to him I would ask Guy, will you? I wanted to hear just from him, yes grace, but never would he answer that way. He would give this long explanation about how long and hard he had worked to provide for me, no one else. He would say, just you, so why do you need to ask me that. I feel that I have had a sheltered life. Having been loved, protected and provided for is my reason for feeling that way. I have in the pass thought of being sheltered, as meaning one being guarded, hindered or prevented from something desired. I had many desires and dreams, many of them came true not all by my efforts alone, but by the efforts of others who cared deeply for me.

I am now nearing seventy and I continue to have dreams and hopes, hopes of a better future than the past has been or the present. My memories are to be treasured. They are not as confluent or flowing together as I wish they were before I began writing down on paper my memories, they were all there in my head, but scattered not in chronological order. Memories have surfaced that had not for many years before. I agree with the saying that the brain is a most amazing organ.

I do have a life now, and it has begun to occur to me that life is a stage I am going through. I'm trying to worship our creator as he asks us to. Worshiping God is a primary purpose of life according to what the Bible says in Revelation 4:11. It says that you are worthy Jehovah, even our God, to receive the glory and the honor and the power, because you created all things, and because of you will existed and were created.

That primary purpose of life is also shown by what the Bible writer Micah said in the book by his name in chapter 6 verse 8. It states" He has told you earthly man what is good and what is Jehovah God asking back from you but to exercise justice and love kindness and to be modest in walking with you God.

The phrases "exercise justice and walk modestly with God" I reason that action is required on my part. So I try to stay busy regularly, doing personal Bible study, attending Christian meetings or engaging in the disciple making work. This is something that is ongoing, not something I will complete or retire from.

About the comforter I was making, I started a month ago to make a comforter. It's a special one never before have I made one like this. Inside each block that is made are feathers. About seventy years ago Mama was still alive and crating things out of whatever was available.

When she would kill a chicken from our yard, she saved he feathers from the body part of the chicken, not the feathers on the wings. They were saved for the purpose of making pillows for beds. She one time saved enough to make a mattress.

About fifty years ago my father gave me two for the pillows that Mama had made. I never used them to sleep on because they were like keep sakes in memory of my parents. This special comforter that I am making in each block I make I put a handful of those feathers in it. When I look in my hand at those feathers I cannot find the words to describe how I feel. My feelings get all mixed up, I get sad because Mama cannot know how I am using those feathers, but I hope one day after the resurrection I can tell her about what I did with the old feathers.

Back in Tuskegee

In 2004 I moved back to Tuskegee Alabama. I moved away from Tuskegee to my hometown of Roanoke Alabama to live. Only one close relative lived there, my brother Lepolion and he was at that time in very bad health. He died soon after I moved there.

I often went to my parent's home and farm. It was about five miles from Roanoke. That made me feel close to them somehow. After Lepolion died there was only three of the fourteen offspring of Lessie and Mollie Smedley left: Lillie, Oliver and myself. We then decided to sale our parent's house and farm.

More than twenty years had passed since any of the land had been cultivated so many trees had grown over the farm land. When preparing to sell the farm I felt such sadness. Papa and Mama had worked so hard to make a living for themselves and to pay for it. Selling the farm was not a problem. In that county there were men who operated sawmills. They cut down trees and made them into lumber for building purposes. Other workers that cut trees for pulp wood to be made into paper wanted the land. So we had no problem getting a buyer. We sold the homeplace at an auction.

During the time I lived in Roanoke, I thought very seriously about getting married. During the twelve years that I lived there two men at two different times talked to me, one in person for about two weeks and the other for about 6 months on the telephone. We talk about our likes and dislikes to see if our values would become compatible, but it did not happen. I wanted to become a wife to a husband again. I very much miss being married.

I was in my sixties during that time. I guess I had gotten too old. About three or four years ago, my older sister Lille had a massive stroke that left her almost completely paralyzed. At that time her husband and his daughter were dead, and she lived alone. I brought her from a hospital in Columbus, Ohio, to my home in Roanoke, Alabama. She never had children of her own so she would have been sent from the hospital to a nursing home. For that reason I brought her home with me to care for her.

She was already eighty-five years old. I first took her to a hospital in Opelika, Alabama, to get some physical therapy. There, therapists worked with her for 30 days. The doctor in Ohio thought it might help her regain some strength and some use of her legs and arms. It did not help her at all. She experienced pain every day and night.

At first for two weeks, her doctor in Opelika would not order a hospital bed for her. After leaving the hospital, I thought she would fall out of the bed without one. The nurse that could have made that possible told me that I would have to watch her day and night and when she gets too close to the edge of the bed, to pull her back to the middle of it. I could watch her through the day, but not all night.

She was only home with me a few days before she did fall out of the bed. I could not pick her up. I thought if I moved her that I might hurt her even more than the fall had done. I called the paramedics and they came and took her to the emergency room. She was examined and x-rayed. It was determined that no bones were broken and she said it did not make her pains any worse. About two days later a hospital bed was sent to my home for her. Throughout the night the leg that she could move, she would push it through the rails on the bed and somehow could not get it out and that caused distress and pain for her. I put a monitor in her room and one in my room. When she needed me or was in distress, I could hear her and then wake up to go and help her.

After I brought her from the hospital she continued to experience pain, her medicine did not help her at all. Lillie wanted everyday to die, she knew if she died she would no longer feel pain, and would be able to rest; and when God's Kingdom started to rule the earth, she hoped and looked forward to being resurrected along with our parents.

During the time she lived with me after the stroke, I learned many things about my sister that I never knew. I had not lived in the same state as she since I was six years old. Now when she came to live with me, I was then seventy-one and she was eighty-five. When Lillie got married she and her husband came to visit for a few days only once a year. After our parents died she came home even less.

One of the reasons she did not come often was that she hated Alabama. Once while her husband was still alive, they came down for a few days. Our niece Kaye sent them both tickets so they could take a plane and not have to drive. After getting the free trip down to visit me and my family along with a dozen or more nieces and nephews she told me while driving them back to Atlanta that she would never come back to Alabama again.

Now she is back in Alabama and very sick. That circumstance for her was another reason she wanted to die. I would ask Lillie sometimes how could she hate this state that our parents worked hard every day to provide for us, all fourteen of us they never lived in any other place. I would say to her if I lived some other place for many years that I would always call Alabama my home.

I will not say that Lillie or any of my other siblings did not love our parents but I do not think they valued them the way they had to provide for us, digging in the dirt in the fields for all of the food we needed, the clothes that we needed, Mama had to make not on an electric sewing machine but on a peddle type one. Sometimes when Mama made sheets and bed-spreads, which required a lot of straight sewing she would say my legs are so tired they are aching.

She would then ask one of us children to sit on the floor in back of the machine and peddle the machine for her. That would allow her legs to get some rest and ease the pain in her legs. One of my brothers and I was talking about Mama and Papa, I mentioned to him that Mama never had a washing machine. I reminded him of all of the water that had to be drawn up from the well for her.

When we were in school or in the field and she did our washing, she drew the water from the well and she got up wood to make a fire under a big iron wash pot. Once the clothes has been washed by hand and a rub board to help remove the dirt from the clothes she put them in the iron pot where the water would be boiling and clean them some more.

If some pieces did not come clean in the pot, she then carried them over to a wood block, laid them on it and beat them with a stick. All of this was her way and only way to get the clothes and other things clean. My brother said to me Grace, Lepolion and I would sometimes get the water for Mama and for us it was fun.

I reminded him, you haven't done nearly as much as Mama has done having fourteen children.

That is only one other reason I feel my siblings did not value our parents. Mama would sometimes say to us you all need to help me more because she would say I am not a machine, I'm human. When I began writing I would call her my sister on the phone and read to her what I was writing about. She then said to me you can use my name if you want. She never explained to me why he thought it was so wrong to write about our life. After I began to understand a little of her thinking, though she never said it but she was ashamed of the way our parents provided for us. I think if Lillie had our Mama's skin color she would have tried to pass as white and gone to a northern state where she was not known and pretend to be white.

Now, when I think about my sister's dislike for Alabama I suppose she did have reasons for the way she felt. After she came to live with me I began to learn things about her that I did not know. I did not grow up with Lillie as I did with my sister Gertrude. I was only six years old when she married and left home. She and her husband Thomas left Alabama soon after they married. They moved to the state of West Virginia. Thomas expected to get a job in one of the coal mines there. Thomas did get the job he wanted, he worked there for the rest of his life. Afterward they would come home to visit only once a year. Seeing her once a year she was pretty much a stranger to me.

When I was in the eleventh grade, she left her husband there in West Virginia and came home. She told our parents that she left her husband because she no longer loved Thomas. If she had other reasons for leaving her husband, I do not know what they were. She continued to live with us for about two months. While she was with us she wanted Mama to change her way of cooking and let her teach her to cook her way. Papa did not like or allow her to do that. He reminded Lille that "Your Mom has cooked for me and our fourteen children for many years and did not need her to tell her how to cook". He also told her when you raise fourteen children and you come home and tell Mollie how you cook for them.

At that time Lillie had no children and never had any. After a few weeks of living with us she went to West Point, Georgia to try to find a job. I don't think she found one because she came back home after about two months. A few weeks later she decided to go to Columbus, Ohio and find a job there. That was around 1947 or 48.
Lillie met a man there named Clinton Hodges and married him soon after she went to Columbus. Her marriage to Thomas lasted for many years, but not so to Clinton. In the 1950's she met and

married William Russ. Her marriage to William (Bud) as he was called lasted until he died in 1994. Lillie continued to live in Columbus until she got sick in 2001. I went to Columbus and brought her home with me where she lived only 16 months before she died.

I begin this putting of my memories down in writing about fifteen years ago. Now at the age of 82, I am going to try to have it published. I continue to have so many memories, especially of my husband and my parents, but I will save them for another time.